Thomas Merton

A Book
of
Hours

A Book of Hours reveals in ways I have never experienced the hidden wellspring of Merton's contemplative life and art. This is a gorgeous book, beautifully conceived and intelligently executed. Deignan has woven a tapestry of Merton's prayer, prose, and poetry at their most ardent so as to re-educate our awareness that God is Beautiful and most worthy of our daily praise. This five-star book will snugly fit the pocket of your heart.

JONATHAN MONTALDO
Editor of *A Year with Thomas Merton*

What a delight to contemplate Thomas Merton's *A Book of Hours*, compiled from the monk's enormous corpus of prose and poetry. Kathleen Deignan's selections and commentary draw the reader ever deeper into the mystery of God's love. A treasure trove to be prayerfully savored.

BR. PATRICK HART
A monk of Gethsemani and Merton's last secretary

Open any page of this wonderful book and you will find a mind-stopping, heart-catching phrase that will remind you, in Merton's unique way, that God is here, all around, right now, and in that moment everything will be different and you will be changed.

SYLVIA BOORSTEIN
Author of *It's Easier Than You Think*

A Book of Hours is faithful to the spirit of Thomas Merton, to the liturgy of hours, and to the One who is our heart's desire. The result is a contemporary psalter that holds us day after day in the embrace of Mystery.

MARY MARGARET FUNK, OSB
Author of *Humility Matters*

THOMAS MERTON

A BOOK

of

HOURS

edited by KATHLEEN DEIGNAN *with a foreword by* JAMES FINLEY

illustrations by JOHN GIULIANI

SORIN BOOKS  Notre Dame, Indiana

The copyright acknowledgments may be found on page 221.

www.sorinbooks.com

ISBN-10 1-933495-05-7 ISBN-13 978-1-933495-05-7

Illustrations by John Giuliani

Cover and text design by Katherine Robinson Coleman

Printed and bound in the United States of America.

Library of Congress Cataloging-in-Publication Data
    Merton, Thomas, 1915-1968.
      A book of hours / Thomas Merton ; edited by Kathleen Deignan; illustrations by John Giuliani ; with a foreword by Jim Finley.
        p. cm.
      Includes bibliographical references.
      ISBN-13: 978-1-933495-05-7
      ISBN-10: 1-933495-05-7
      1. Devotional literature. I. Deignan, Kathleen, 1947- II. Title.

    BV4832.3.M47 2007
    242'.2—dc22

                                        2006033696

FOR ALL THOSE
WE MOVE THROUGH
TIME WITH,
AND ALL THOSE
WHO BECKON
FROM ETERNITY.

C⊙ntents

....

his book, imagined and brought forth by Kathleen Deignan, gathers together some of the most beautiful and insightful passages in the writings of Thomas Merton arranged as prayers to be offered at the dawn, midday, dusk, and night hours of each day. The result is a contemporary version of the ancient form of prayer book called a Book of Hours. You will have to find out for yourself how using this Book of Hours might enhance your own spiritual journey. But sometimes by swapping stories, we who journey together on the spiritual path can encourage and help one another along. In this spirit, then, I will share with you how the spiritual path embodied in this book continues to transform my life.

I first began to read Thomas Merton in 1958. Being only fourteen years old at the time, I was too young to appreciate much of what Merton was saying. But I was able to sense that Merton's words about God came from his own deep experience of God. In a vague but sincere way, I sensed that reading Thomas Merton might help me find my way to God. When I graduated from high school I entered the Trappist monastery of the Abbey of Gethsemani in Kentucky, where Merton lived. My master plan was to enter the monastery so that Merton might guide me in my search for God. And, amazingly enough, that is just what happened. As a novice under Merton's care in his role as master of novices, I met with Merton on a regular basis for one-on-one spiritual direction.

What I treasure the most in my moments with Merton is not any specific thing he said. Rather, what I treasure most is that everything he said amounted to an invitation to join him in listening to God in silence. It is this invitation that I hear in each passage of this book. I hope that as you pray with this book, you will hear Merton extending this invitation to you as well, inviting you to listen in silence, surrender to the silence, discover for yourself how patiently God waits in silence for all your inner noise to exhaust itself, so that, finally, impoverished and spent, you can begin to hear God uttering you and all things into being.

You do not have to search very hard to discover this invitation to listen that reverberates in everything that Merton says. You will discover this call to listen as you slowly linger with his word, so as not to pass right over the hidden treasure he invites you to discover. What is so disarming is that as you learn to listen you begin to realize this treasure is God's very presence within you, uttering you into being as someone God eternally treasures.

As we learn to read Merton in this way, the pauses between the sentences become longer. The silence, engendered by a single thought-stopping phrase, deepens. In this attentive silence we begin to realize that God's still, small voice, reverberating in Merton's words, is reverberating within ourselves and within every passing hour of our lives. This, then, is the spirit in which I hope you sit with the prayers, poems, and psalms of Thomas Merton—not looking simply for information, nor even for inspiration, but rather for the stop-dead-in-your-track one-liners that send you falling into the depths of silence you cannot name or claim or understand.

Sitting with Merton's writings in this way, you just might begin to sense that he is speaking directly to you when he says:

> It is not easy to try and say what I know I cannot say. I do really have the feeling that you have seen something most precious—and most available too. The reality that is present to us and in us: Call it Being, call it Atman, call it Pneuma . . . or Silence. And the simple fact that by being attentive, by learning to listen (or recovering the natural capacity to listen which cannot be learned any more than breathing), we can find ourselves engulfed in such happiness that it cannot be explained: the happiness of being at one with everything that is hidden in the ground of Love for which there can be no explanations. I suppose what makes me most glad is that we recognize each other in this metaphysical space of silence and happiness, and get some sense, for a moment, that we are "full of paradise without knowing it."[1]

We do not know we are full of paradise because we are so full of our own noise that we cannot hear God singing us and all things into being. And so Merton shows us the way home. He surrenders to God in silence. He surrenders so completely to God's silence that when he begins to speak, his voice and God's voice merge in a polyphony of grace and glory that causes our own heart to begin to stir and awaken.

It is at this juncture that we can appreciate how the content of this book so seamlessly merges with its structure as a Book of Hours. For it is hour by hour that we learn to hear the polyphony of God reverberating in everything we hear. It is hour by hour we learn not to believe in and blurt out the off key comments that come out of the exiled places in our own head. It is hour by hour that we come to discover that the apparent cacophony of phones ringing, of traffic going by, of so many people saying so many things, is the polyphony of God's voice reverberating in the world. As we learn to recognize and listen to this polyphony, we are transformed. As we are transformed, we begin to realize that "we are full of paradise without knowing it."

And so here you are holding in your hands a way to join Merton on the listening path. I sense Thomas Merton is somehow nearby, waiting in each thing he says to encourage you not to doubt all that God might achieve in you, all that God might express through you, as you surrender to God in silence.

JAMES FINLEY

ACKN⊙WLEDGMENTS

Thanks are due to many who have supported this labor: Anne McCormick, Director of the Merton Trust; Brother Patrick Hart and the Community of Gethsemani for their warm welcome and encouragement during my visit; Judith Kubicki, CSSF, and Jaculyn Hanrahan, CND, for their insight into the form of the Hours, and to Meg Funk, OSB, for her deep understanding of the practice of *lectio divina*; to Patricia Roldan, my research assistant for her invaluable help; and all the people at Sorin Books who brought this book to form, especially Bob Hamma and Peter Gehred.

I am grateful for the encouragement of the sisters and associates of the Congregation of Notre Dame, especially Jeanne Fielder, CND, and Jacquline Greenfield. Thanks to my colleagues in the Department of Religious Studies at Iona College, and for the virtual and global community of those who have found in Merton a true spiritual master. In this regard I would especially like to thank Paul Pearson, Jonathan Montaldo, and the members of the International Thomas Merton Society as well as the Merton societies of Canada, of Great Britain and Ireland, and of the Low Countries. I thank, too, all the young Merton scholars—especially Daniel, Kimberly, and Victor—whose enthusiasm for his legacy ensures another generation of disciples. And for the inspiration and support of my sister Ann Deignan, herself a poet, who was creating her first play as this book unfolded.

Special gratitude to Father John Giuliani and Jim Finley whose creativity graces this book.

And to Merton the psalmist, the man of praise, unending thanks. With him I have prayed each word in the preparation of this beautiful breviary, that it be a blessing for all who take it up and mark their days and hours with its poetry, its different wisdom and grace.

KATHLEEN DEIGNAN, CND
BELTAINE 2006

*There must be a time of day when the man who
makes plans forgets his plans,
and acts as if he had no plans at all.*

*There must be a time of day when the man who has
to speak falls very silent.
And his mind forms no more propositions,
and he asks himself:
Did they have a meaning?*

*There must be a time
when the man of prayer goes to pray
as if it were the first time in his life
he had ever prayed,
when the man of resolutions puts his
resolutions aside
as if they had all been broken,
and he learns a different wisdom:*

*distinguishing the sun from the moon,
the stars from the darkness,
the sea from the dry land,
and the night sky from the shoulder of a hill.[1]*

Thi s is a Book of Hours for those who desire to learn "a different wisdom" taught by the contemplative master Thomas Merton, of attending to those times of the day when we might set our work aside, fall silent, and begin to pray. In 1941 at the age of twenty-six, Merton sought refuge in the Trappist monastery of Our Lady of Gethsemani, Kentucky, "in revolt against the meaningless confusion of a life in which there was so much activity, so much movement, so much useless talk, so much superficial and needless stimulation," that he could not remember who he was.[2] For the next half of his life he learned a new way of being, supported by a rhythmic pattern of daily prayer that aided the recovery and discovery of a new self, his true self, drawn up like a jewel from seas of confusion, restlessness, and banality.

Plagued by the same questions and afflictions that torment people of our time, Thomas Merton lived deeply into "a different wisdom" of the healing, illuminating, and transformative Christian mysteries. His passion was to share this wisdom with those of us beyond the monastic enclosure. Not that he had found answers, but he had discerned a way to plumb the more radical questions that have engaged spiritual seekers from the beginning of time. He understood his vocation to be a servant of the human quest for meaning, transcendence, and communion—an explorer in realms of the human heart few of us dare to probe. In this wilderness of soul Merton discovered not only the self he had lost in the maze of the modern world, but its deeper source: the loving depths of divine mystery. In recovering his own soul, he found himself whole, well, and sane, and he taught routes to this fundamental wholeness, discovered by the awakening of the contemplative mind. Once disoriented in a desiccating anguish and confusion of the world's and his own making, he came in time to know the peace of one who had found his way home—to God, to the world, to himself.

The experiential contact with the Living God encompassed Merton on all sides: in the glories of nature, the pathos of society, in the stimulating conversations with countless dialogue partners across the planet, and in the monastic liturgy of ceaseless prayer. In time his life itself became inexhaustible adoration fueled by a rapture that overflowed in endless expressions of praise, sounding in the solitude and silence that were his dwelling place in the woodlands of Appalachia. From his forest abode whose doors and windows were ever open to the world, he spent his days in intercession for us all, composing a body of "different wisdom" shared in his extraordinary legacy of spiritual and social writings. In this place he marked the hours of the passing days and nights and seasons. He lived into their beauty and anguish, their grace and wisdom, gathering it all for us as guidance, orientation, inspiration, and instruction in the sacred mysteries of human transformation. And so he remains, decades after his death, the master of prayer, because he was himself a master of praise.

"Songs grow up around me like a jungle. Choirs of all creatures sing the tunes Your Spirit played in Eden."[3]

Praise has ever been the preoccupation of those who live in vital awareness of a universe resplendent with mystery. From the dawn of our creation, humankind has generated visionaries who communicate a sense of the sacred. These mystic artists, poets, dramatists, liturgists, and symbolists inspire an extraordinary creativity in response to the numinous dimension of being, empowering us to live within it with courage, reverence, and awe. From the earliest aboriginal patterns of naked stammering before the raw power of nature, to the highly stylized rituals of the classical religions played out in temples buttressed by elaborate metaphysical and theological underpinnings—every society has found its way to pray and order the day in a deepening consciousness of the ineffable dimensions of mystery, by whatever name. The monotheisms, polytheisms, henotheisms, and atheisms that play at naming and unnaming the Holy Unnamable create a chorus of mystical languages by which humankind celebrates its religious awareness. Whether in magical songs of the shamans of early human communities, or the sacred Vedas and mantras of Hinduism, the chanting of Buddhists in their meditation halls, or the cries of the muezzin from towering minarets summoning Muslims to prayer—the earth resounds with a symphony of songs that sing of a different wisdom inviting us to praise. And perhaps the most familiar and enduring of such songs are the psalms.

"When psalms surprise me with their
music and antiphons turn to rum
the bottom drops out of my soul."[4]

Thomas Merton considered the Hebrew Book of Psalms the most significant and influential collection of religious poems ever written. Dialogical in nature, they express the discourse of faith between the people of the Covenant and their God, and as a body of sacred literature they comprise the most insightful theological and liturgical resource given us in the biblical tradition. "Seven times a day do I praise you" declares the Hebrew psalmist, remembering with each song the alternating hours and seasons of well-being and anguish that are the life of faith. Written by the finest poets in Israel for the liturgy of the Temple, and originally accompanied by skillful musicians on lyre and harp, the psalms intone all the emotions of human experience: praise, complaint, awe, grief, adoration, penitence, gratitude, and surprise at the gratuitous bounty and mercy of the Living God. These soul-songs of the Jewish community were the very prayers and songs of Jesus, too, which he sang from dawn to dark, marking the hours of his days, giving spirit to the feasts, festivals, and pilgrimages he celebrated with his friends, and which echoed in the words of his world-changing gospel. In time these same psalms became the universal songs of exultation, lamentation, and wonder sung by the community his Spirit brought into being, inspiring its own liturgy and scriptures.

THE WORK OF PRAISE: *Opus Dei*

"The Hours sustain me."[5]

All Christian worship echoes the sacred poetry of praise and pathos of the psalms, which provide the reverberating core of the Church's daily prayer. From the Church's earliest days, sounding the psalms at morning and evening were the two resonant chords of prayer, often elaborated by "little hours" in between, as a way to honor the admonition of Paul "to pray without ceasing."[6] Indeed the psalms and hymns and inspired songs contained much of the Church's seminal theology, giving the emotional tonality and relational sensibility to its God-language and worship. Following the Empire's work *horarium*, and in response to the forum bells, urban Christian communities of the Roman *imperium* established a prayer schedule, marking the passage of the day with nominated hours of prayer. Whether assembled at designated gathering places for communal worship, domestically in the intimacy of family circles, or in solitary devotion, the psalms were the privileged prayer of Christians giving common voice to their faithfulness. By the third century even the deserts of the Middle East silently resounded with melodious psalms as the earliest monastics let flow a torrent that became a ceaseless tide of vivifying praise turning barren lands into gardens of encounter with the living God. By the sixth century Benedict, the father of western monasticism, had given ceaseless prayer its grid in a *horarium* that metered the sacred work—the *"opus Dei"*—of the monk by set hours.

The Divine Office, as the labor of regular prayer is called, celebrates the formative Benedictine vision that the work of prayer, expressed in chanting the psalms, is the central human activity of the monk (*"orare est laborare"*); and the prayer of work (*"laborare est orare"*) is its mindful extension throughout the day. As the Christian tradition evolved, the great work of ceaseless prayer was supported by the performative structures of the cathedral and monastic offices. Eventually on into the middle ages, more devotional and private prayer manuals such as the Book of Hours were designed to sustain the contemplative prayer of lay Christians. As monastic and other spiritual communities arose in their manifold variety, notably Merton's own Cistercian order, they used the psalms to compose a liturgy of time, designing the day as ceaseless psalmody in praise of the Mystery.

The Way of Praise: *Lectio Divina*

"The pleasure of reading . . . 'helps me Godward.'"[7]

As a monk in the Cistercian tradition Thomas Merton's life was spent in singing and praying the psalms. They were the form of his unceasing prayer, and he treasured them as bread in the wilderness for the Christian soul, sustenance for the religious imagination. He made a promise to pray a "perpetual Psalter . . . from now until I die" as his form of communion with all his spiritual ancestors who from time immemorial voiced these songs.[8] He taught that the Psalter was a school of contemplation opening up surprising depths for those who know how to enter them, "a marvelous and inexhaustible actuality."[9] He encouraged us to sing the psalms, meditate on them, use them in all the happenings of our spiritual life, particularly in the liturgy, which is the school of the interior life in the Christian way.

But he was also fond of other varieties of "psalms"— poetries of the sacred from across traditions and cultures, both ancient and contemporary. As a sacred poet himself, his sense of what comprised a contemplative psalter was generous and eclectic, as he sought in the strange and wonderful tongues of mystics world-wide new ways to spell divine praise: "the pleasure of reading and writing poetry . . . 'helps me Godward'."[10]

Extraordinary literary artist that he was, Merton had a remarkable capacity for *lectio divina*—sacred reading, or reading a text in a sacred way. Practiced by all religious traditions that prize their scriptures, the art of *lectio divina* is essential to biblical faiths which honor the word as a medium of divine revelation. In the Christian tradition, *lectio divina* is the very foundation of our experience of worship and its reverberation in the silence of contemplative life. But the scope of *lectio* is wide and deep, because the nature of the word is the same. Merton knew well that the Word of God is not only being uttered in the sacred scriptures, but more primordially in creation, more existentially in history, more imaginatively in works of art, more immediately and personally in human experience. Because he perceived the dimensionality of the Word of God he understood how to read it in all its myriad forms.

Thomas Merton raised up the ancient practice of *lectio divina* as a distinctly Christian way of reading scripture as a resource for the contemplative life by returning to the teachings of the early spiritual masters who sought the many voices stored in those revelatory texts. The deeply personal practice of *lectio* unfolds in four non-linear movements that oscillate between the sensuous experience of *kataphatic* forms conveyed in words and images and the *apophatic* experience of a pregnant emptiness beyond all sense and reason. In this approach *lectio* proper is the reading of the "text" of creation, of events, of art, of personal experience, or of scripture—sacred and secular—in a slow, thoughtful and reflective way, perusing the text before us in all its imaginal richness. The second movement is *meditatio*, which suggests ruminating over the text—words or images—either by repetition, recitation, or memorization, which allows us to hold the text and be held by it in mindful awareness. The third movement is *oratio*, our prayerful expression of heartfelt gratitude, praise, remorse, or petition in response to the movement of the savored word in our consciousness. And *contemplatio*, is our soulful resting in the presence of Mystery, which has stirred in the poetic images of the text, and has awakened us and moved us beyond all words, images, and concepts toward a quiet abiding in wordless silence.

This practice of *lectio* is often described in metaphors of feasting and eating, because the Word of God—in all the various modalities noted above—is the soul food of the mystical life. Merton speaks of the sweetness of *lectio*, and of the delight which tasting and savoring, chewing, and metabolizing divine wisdom offers: "for me it seems better to read almost anything and everything."[11] How necessary, then, to learn to read the revelatory texts of scripture, sunsets, heartbreaks, aesthetic works, benedictions and catastrophe, prose and prophecy, and all the other miraculous and perplexing "words of God" endlessly being storied forth for our deep reading. They all invite our skillfull practice of the art *lectio divina*, one of the primary modalities of Christian transformation that brings us, in both our waking and dreaming, to the wellsprings of contemplation, the ground of our life of praise.

THE GROUND OF PRAISE: THE CONTEMPLATIVE SELF

> *"May my bones burn and ravens eat my flesh,*
> *If I forget thee, contemplation!"*[12]

What Thomas Merton discovered in the Abbey of Gethsemani he desired to share with the whole world: a deeply experiential life in God that is the gift of our creation, the very reason we were born, a grace available to everyone. It meant for him "the search for truth and for God . . . finding the true significance of my life and my right place in God's creation."[13] Merton taught that the contemplative journey toward the indwelling and all encompassing God is made on the existential pathways of one's own self. The search for the One is the discovery of the Other in a transformative encounter with the divine image and presence at the core of our true self.

Yet, as Merton faithfully reminded us, everyone is shadowed by a false or illusory self who wants to exist outside the reach of God's will and love, outside of reality and life. This counterfeit and evanescent creation is dedicated to the narcissistic cult of its own shadow in self-orbiting liturgies of egocentric adulation, ordering all things in its universe around itself. Over and over Merton warns us that the only true joy on earth is to escape from the prison of this disturbing stranger who occupies our psyche, and enter by love "into union with the Life Who dwells and sings within the essence of every creature and in the core of our own souls."[14] To live in this conscious communion is what Merton means by contemplative life that plants in us something of heaven.

Contemplative life, therefore, begins with the recovery of one's natural unity, a reintegration of our compartmentalized, colonized, traumatized, technologically entranced, and workaholic being. We must gather our fragmented selves from our distracted, exhausted, noise polluted, and frenzied existence, so that when we say "I" there is actually a unified human person present to support that pronoun. But this is only the preliminary work of salvation, because the deep transcendent self is a divine creature, shy and wild, secret and spontaneous, preferring the silence and humility of a pure heart in which to make its mysterious appearance. This true self "must be drawn up like a jewel from the bottom of the sea,"[15] by a steady work of descent to recover the immortal diamond in whose every facet is reflected the invisible face of God.

Contemplation, then, is a gradual interiorizing of consciousness, a going inside to quiet our minds, calm our hearts, and move toward deeper levels of our own nature. It is aided by regular intervals of silence and solitude, stillness and serenity that allow our lives to be listening to the ever-speaking mystery of God. Merton reminds us that while our existence is noisy, our essential being is silent: beneath the clamor of our chaotic lives there is a resonant ground of silence. In this rich silence—the silence of God—we taste the sweetness of our own souls, the peace of our own hearts. Merton encourages us to take every opportunity to feed on this silence, soak it into our bones so that we might hear the divine One say in us: "I am." The contemplative discovers that the secret of our identity is hidden and revealed in the love and mercy of God. There is nothing else worth living for, "only this infinitely peaceful love Who is beyond words, beyond emotion, beyond intelligence."[16]

In this sudden awakening, we come to realize that all of reality is swimming in meaning, charged with the glory of divinity. More intimately, we discover that love is our authentic nature, our true destiny, a personal revolution that energizes *a certain special way of being alive.*[17] It is for this self-transcendence and communion that we exist, becoming the likeness of the One whose image we are: radiant centers of reconciling love, extending the circumference of mercy and care throughout the earth. In that likeness we become peacemakers, justice builders, caretakers of creation, and witnesses to the sufficiency of the next breath and heartbeat, of each familiar and friend, in a world gone mad for money and power and things. Such contemplative traction aids us in resisting the vertigo of our times, which would pull us of off course in the various storms of history.

In Merton's teaching, contemplation is the practice of supreme mindfulness and care. Yet, paradoxically, its fruit is a serene carelessness, as we are progressively freed from self-preoccupation and neurotic concern; we are allowed to live without the paralyzing anxiety that would extend its rule to our souls. There is no need for harried, hurried vexation. God is hidden within, and all things that are not a means of bringing the heart to this tranquility in the divine will are useless. This is the fruit of contemplative praise that arises from the hidden ground of love: the discovery of God in the discovery of our true self, and in that love which is the reality of both God and self, to embrace the world.

The Master of Praise: Merton the Psalmist

"The windows are open. Let the psalms fly in."[18]

Thomas Merton spent his life writing about contemplation, yet his own way of prayer was in fact surprisingly simple, "centered entirely on attention to the presence of God and to His will and His love . . . a kind of *praise* rising up of out of the center of Nothing and Silence . . . not thinking about anything, but a direct seeking of the Face of the Invisible."[19] Much has been written about Thomas Merton the monk, contemplative, spiritual master, social and ecclesial prophet, pioneer of interfaith dialogue, critic of art, culture, and literature, and of Merton the poet—but not explicitly about Merton the *psalmist*. Yet there is a virtual psalter lacing through his voluminous writings, both poetry and prose, that comprises an elegant and distinctly contemporary voice of Christian praise. He insisted that his own personal task was not simply to be a poet and writer, still less a commentator or pseudo-prophet, but "basically to *praise* God out of an inner center of silence, gratitude and 'awareness' . . . my task is simply the breathing of this gratitude from day to day, in simplicity, and for the rest turning my hand to whatever comes, work being part of praise."[20]

He reports getting out of bed in the middle of the night because it was imperative that he say psalms with his face on the floor, alone, without a woman, in the rapturous embrace of his silent forest bride whose sweet dark warmth was the root of all the secrets lovers knew and that mystics longed to know. The God-intoxicated man had extinguished all but one desire: to be at the house where his love is, in the garden of Paradise. En route there, and arriving there, the songs he sang were the psalms he intoned around the clock, the very breath and heart beat of his Cistercian life.

As Merton's life of psalmody deepened it awakened the psalmist within him as well. He began inscribing new psalms in the poetic prose and countless poems that seemed to flow from the inexhaustible wellsprings of his silence, the original reservoir of authentic human language from which all praise arises and to which it returns. In a cascade of literary eloquence he soon became the unique voice of a contemporary contemplative reawakening, inspiring in his readers a similar hunger for the experience of God. For Merton, poetry was the near horizon of this encounter, because like music and art it attuned the soul to God, inducing contact with the Creator of a universe resplendent with traces of divinity. Poetry was the "free speech" of the new human being, the Christ-self, reborn to Edenic consciousness by the labor of conversion.[21] By creative sympathy and intuitive understanding, Merton found a way into the "hidden wholeness"[22] that informs a sacramental universe pregnant with mystery, a paradisal plane of plenitude. He responded in meteoric bursts of verbal luminosity, celebrating the power of God hiding for all to see in the splendors of creation, and murmuring in the secrecy of the human heart.

As Merton's prose progressively became raids on the unspeakable brutality and violence of our age, his mystical poems were raids on the ineffable. In rich, outrageous, lush, and lavish language he spelled out a vision of existence stunning to the impoverished religious imagination of postmodern Christianity. To the blood soaked soul of the twentieth century languishing in the eclipse of spirit-deadening skepticism and self-consciousness, Merton dared to speak with the innocence of faith: the primordial intuition of original wholeness, meaning, and mercy at the heart of reality. While the "master narrative" of Christianity progressively suffered distortion, discontinuity, and fragmentation throughout his life, Merton was indefatigable in reweaving the threads of the sacred story on the loom of his inspired religious imagination, unapologetic for spinning a yarn to clothe his existential nakedness, a vestment to wear for his everyday liturgies of praise.

Thomas Merton's was a new voice of the wounding and wonder of our world experience, and his verse articulated a fully integrated vision of our time and of its spirit. His poetry had wings, taking flight and soaring above and then beyond the horizon of ordinary God-talk. With it, he enticed his readers to abandon the moribund formulaic renderings of sacred discourse and dared us to become with him psalmists of the new age, to re-enchant a soul-threatened world. He beckoned us to enter the mystic's mind through the "mythos gate" of revelatory speech,[23] assuring us that on the other side of that portal one awakens from a dream state and enters into a new reality through the gate of heaven, which is everywhere.

THE TERRITORY OF PRAISE: "LE POINT VIERGE" OF PARADISE

"This is the burning promised land, the house of God, the gate of heaven."[24]

In the several decades of his monastic life, Thomas Merton became a dervish of praise spinning around a still point of presence manifesting on the surface and in the depths of everything, especially the human heart. He labored to name this mysterious center of being, "a point of nothingness which is untouched by sin and by illusion, a point of pure truth, a point or spark which belongs entirely to God, which is never at our disposal, from which God disposes of our lives, which is inaccessible to the fantasies of our own mind or the brutalities of our own will."[25] He called it "le point vierge"—the "virgin point" of the spirit where one meets God, and which is the glory of God in us. It is like "a pure diamond, blazing with the invisible light of heaven," seen at once in the landscape of a numinous dawn, and the inscape of the heart's secret beauty. It is in everyone and everything, and if we could see it "we would see these billions of points of light coming together in the face and blaze of a sun that would make the darkness and cruelty of life vanish completely." Merton had no program to suggest for this seeing; it was in his experience the wide open secret to which so few attend: "paradise is all around us and we do not understand."[26] But the return to paradise, and the delineation of access routes for its discovery, was the passion of his life.

In accepting the "Edenic office of the poet"[27] Merton labored to celebrate and name this paradisal awareness that awakens in the free speech of intimate conversation with God. He reports that the territory of paradise is here on earth, our original homeland, the undivided simplicity of a God-like consciousness restored to its essential wisdom and compassion. The pathway to paradise is contemplation by which we are lead back to our original nature in quiet praise and gratitude, and to a different wisdom that attunes us to an experience of harmony with all life. For this paradisal existence we were made—for peace, delight, safety, joy, freedom, and the highest spiritual happiness. In it we walk around "shining like the sun,"[28] energized by our intimacy with divinity to do the work of the citizens of paradise—a creative and restorative collaboration to renew the face of the earth. Contemplation makes us God's new paradise, sacraments of hope and signs of contradiction who do not succumb to the world-weariness of our race, but are ever revitalized by joining the cosmic dance in rhythm with the heartbeat of life itself.

THE TIME OF PRAISE: "LE TEMPS VIERGE" OF ETERNITY

"You have given me roots in eternity."[29]

If the territory of paradise is here, it's time is now—each and every seminal moment that plants seeds of spiritual vitality in the human soul. But few of us are receptive to these pregnant germs of grace because we do not sense time as the field of encounter with divine presence. Rather we live in a time of no room, "obsessed with lack of time, lack of space, saving time, conquering space, projecting into time and space the anguish produced within them by the technological furies of size, volume, quantity, speed, number, price, acceleration."[30] There is no room for the mysterious spaciousness of being, no time for presence; no room for nature, no time for quiet, for thought, for presence. We are "worked to the point of insensibility, dazed by information, drugged by entertainment, surfeited with everything, nauseated with the human race, and with ourselves, nauseated with life."[31] We have made time a problem and our language betrays how yet another living mystery has become a commercial commodity to make, take, give, lose, spend, save, share, waste, beat, stretch, manage, and kill. It flies, it drags, it never stands still and our maladaptation to the fact of impermanence, to the ephemeral nature of reality, is a source of real affliction.

We fear the thief of time that steals from us the treasure we did not take the time to discover hidden in the cracks between *chronos*—"a linear flight into nothingness"[32]—and *kairos*—the time of possibility and abundance that opens as we return to the immediacy of what is real. "Be a son of this instant,"[33] Merton advises, because the present is our right place, where the mind is at home. Otherwise it is drawn out of its depths into the illusion to which it tends, exiling us from the present, displacing us in the imaginary, the absent, in a future or past beyond our reach, in the warp-spasm of frenzied acceleration that is the hallmark of our contemporary life.

Although a monk, Merton shared our vexations with time; his journals are replete with confessions of exhaustion at the breathless, often mindless pace and time-fracturing played out even in the monastery. But his gradual entrainment to the liturgy of the hours and days and seasons became a way for him to synchronize his rhythms to the pace of the great wheel of time turning in the circuits of the Christian calendar. Time became a sacrament, a medium of encounter with divinity playing in temporal cycles that opened to the sacred mysteries of life and death and rising in the great round of Christian life. The more his spiritual life deepened, the more he realized that time was no enemy but rather the field in which God meets us. The chronology of Christian life attuned him to the sacred beginnings of the world; it enlightened him to the profound spiritual evolution progressively unfolding, in fits and starts, toward a merciful *eschaton*, a climax of redemption played out in the drama of history. Through Christ, the new human, he moved into that time stream that arises from the deep abyss of God's eternity, and learned to flow home to the source in the timeless One, his soul laden with gifts received in time.

So deeply did Merton learn to treasure time, toward the end of his life he asked to live in a small hermitage on the monastic lands. In this solitude, the seeds of contemplation rooted deeply in the fertile soil of his silent spirit, yielding a harvest of wisdom—the very taste of the sweetness of God. He learned from the provocative masters of the Christian East that such communion could eventually nurture *theosis*—a progressive transformation into God—and he shared this manna with all of his virtual disciples in the world. He learned there in the rounding of his days at Mt. Olivet that time could suddenly stop in a moment of prayer that arrested the soul in the presence of God: "Time no longer means anything in such prayer, which is carried on in instants of its own, instants that can last a second or an hour without our being able to distinguish one from another. For this prayer belongs less to time than to eternity."[34] He learned that *now* is eternity's nearest station, a threshold to the living presence where God is found by sinking into the heart of the moment as it is. He wondered at the grip the present had on him: the reality of *now*, the unreality of all the rest, held in the folds of conscious wakefulness.

What Merton learned, he taught—that the epiphany of God in time can come to us at any moment, anywhere, whether we are praying or not. It can come at work, on the road, in any situation, because it is a deep and secret movement of the divine spirit within our own, the felt sense of God's own self-discovery in us. The life of contemplation prepares us for such intervals of divine encounter, creating a new experience of time: "*le temps vierge*"[35]—one's own time felt at once as abundant fullness and profound emptiness. Like the enigmatic "*point vierge*," its temporal analog is a point of "nowhereness in the middle of movement, a point of nothingness in the midst of being." It is an incomparable point of contact with mystery by which we pass through the center of our own nothingness and enter into infinite reality to awaken as our true self.[36]

Le temps vierge is the time of openness to all that is just as it is. It is healing time when some great and secret mercy works miracles in our woundedness, and so it is *compassionate* time. In this space of liberty, free of the demands of the world and the ego, all possibilities are allowed to surface and new choices become manifest in a moment of pure potential. This is the different wisdom Merton harvested from the seeds of contemplation nurtured in the soil of the present moment, the near frontier of eternity. In his moments of real presence he came to see what is ours to see as well in the *temps vierge* of quiet praise:

> *The world and time are the dance of the Lord*
> *in emptiness.*
> *The silence of the spheres is the music of*
> *a wedding feast.*

> *The more we persist in misunderstanding the phenomena*
> *of life,*
> *the more we analyze them out into strange finalities*
> *and complex purposes of our own,*
> *the more we involve ourselves in sadness, absurdity and*
> *despair.*

But it does not matter much,
because no despair of ours can alter the
reality of things,
or stain the joy of the cosmic dance which is always
there.

Indeed we are in the midst of it,
and it is in the midst of us,
for it beats in our very blood, whether we
want it to or not.

Yet the fact remains that we are invited to forget
ourselves on purpose,
cast our awful solemnity to the winds and join in the
general dance.[37]

THE HORARIUM OF PRAISE: *A Book of Hours*

"Prime each morning makes me safe and free.
The Day Hours sustain me with their economy,
by night I am buried in Christ."[38]

Though the man of quiet praise wrote inexhaustibly about prayer, he did not create a book of prayer for those of us he summoned to contemplation. Yet the ingredients for such a book are embedded in Merton's voluminous corpus of writings on the mystical life, social and political concerns, the arts, and the natural world. He leaves us a literary legacy rich with sacred poetry, and with "found" psalms, hymns, and canticles ready to become elements of a breviary to sustain the prayer life of worldly Christians.

This, then, is such a book composed entirely of Merton's scriptures: his glosses on the texts of divine revelation speaking in nature, scripture, history, culture, and his own heart. It takes its inspiration from the most popular book of the middle ages, the Book of Hours, designed to nurture the spiritual life of lay Christians. These early breviaries contained the prayers, psalms, and intercessions with which the devout kept their daily appointments with mystery. Works of art in themselves, they were inscribed as beautifully illuminated manuscripts designed to engage the aesthetic senses, even as the spiritual senses awakened in *lectio divina*. Likewise, this Book of Hours composed of Merton's prayer, invites the modern engaged contemplative to discover a different wisdom awaiting us as we keep our appointments with mystery at the stations of dawn, day, dusk, and dark in a pattern of praise that awakens our contemplative self.

Merton was once asked by an enquirer how he lived a day in his monastic hermitage. In his celebrated essay, "Day of a Stranger,"[39] he describes the passage of the hours enlightened by the sun's movement from horizon to horizon illuminating a world resplendent with divine presence manifested in beings near and far. He names his neighbors and familiars that comprised the natural and mental ecology of his woodland world: rain and crows, poets, and mystics and prophets of all times and places with whom he formed a community of soul. Elsewhere he tells how it was necessary that he experience all the times and moods of his one good place and about receiving from the Eastern woods, the single word DAY spoken in a new language each dawn; and in yet another place he tells of sitting in darkness to hear the eloquent night. He confesses singing the fiery songs of prophets loud across hills being ravaged by polluters, and to chanting psalms softly toward the paradise tree, the cosmic axle that grew cruciform in the garden he lived in with God. As darkness descended on his valley, he poured out his prayer on a world that seemed intent upon destruction.

Merton was entrained by monastery bells to attend to the stations of hourly prayer in the pattern of the monastic canonical office. But he also worked to create a *horarium* in sync with his own personal rhythms and flow, and encouraged the engaged contemplatives he wrote for to do the same. He realized that contemplation in a world of action requires different support from what monastics know in their regular hours of prayer fixed in time and text. Rather, he urged secular contemplatives to be creative in learning ways to stop the world and stop the clock in order to enter into the *temps vierge* of prayer.

Merton suggested we give ourselves the benefit of those parts of the day that are quiet because the world does not value them, like the small hours of the morning, and the silent hours of darkness when we can hear night pouring down her canticles of deepest praise. In between there are the day hours of labor as we turn toward the world, each doing our part to build the earth. These hours are also funded by quiet praise, free of care and anxiety, marked by a cultivated mindfulness that has trained us to perceive the presence of divinity everywhere and always. These daylight hours ground our prayer in work and our work in prayer, consecrating our labor for the life of the world. At evening we come home again to the familiar place where our soul lives, ready to give thanks, and then at night to sink into the darkness of mystery.

This Book of Hours honors the Christian practice of celebrating Sunday, the dominical feast, as the first day of the New Creation which brings eternity into time. Imbued by the grace and power of the Sabbath, we are invited to turn toward the world as the week unfolds, to repair, heal, and build the earth as the realm of divine mercy and love. As Sunday begins the week in exultant praise, Saturday ends it in a Marian mood of quiet contemplation. This day is composed of two of Merton's most exquisite meditations. From dawn till dusk we are invited by *Hagia Sophia* to move into the feminine dimension of mystery, coursing through the fluidity of time borne by the single motif of Wisdom hidden and revealing everywhere. At dark, we spend the last hour of the week accompanying Merton on his mystical "Fire Watch."

Thomas Merton's *A Book of Hours* is a prayer book and more. It is a catechesis of the Christian life, a manual of mysticism, a psalter, a set of teachings for engaged contemplatives, a guide for the formation of conscience, a collection of *koans* and *mantras* and breath prayers, a gospel. Such is the wealth he has left us in his inexhaustible legacy of spiritual writing. Although there are but seven days in this collection, the richness of every hour affords far more than is necessary for each contemplative station. In the slow pace of *lectio* one can expect to get arrested by a word or image, an exhortation or antiphon, and be drawn into the timelessness of *"le temps vierge."* In this way this little breviary will be an endless source of inspiration as we return to it day by day, hour by hour discovering some new and unexpected turn of phrase to ignite our souls to quiet praise.

Notes on Praying *A Book of Hours*

This Book of Hours is composed to help us enter the *temps vierge* of prayer, into that incomparable point of contact with mystery by which we pass through the center of our own nothingness and enter into the infinite reality of our true selves in God. There is no set hour ascribed for each of the four prayer stations—*dawn, day, dusk, dark*—since each of us has different rhythms of waking and working, resting and retiring. Rather we are invited to let this breviary serve our soul-needs on any given day, using just what hours we are able, and even within any given hour, just what elements hold us for the time we have. Find a quiet, inviting place to let your soul open to the Presence Who is ever present. Find your way into your own silence, no matter what the world is offering you at the moment. Begin to center using your slow and steady breathing to conduct you toward that inner horizon, that *point vierge* of emptiness, openness, and spaciousness that is your own deeper nature. Then let yourself begin. As James Finley has suggested, these prayers offer us far more in each hour than the soul needs—here, as in many other things, less is more.

This Book of Hours is composed of familiar elements of Christian liturgy and is supportive of both solitary and communal prayer—all drawn from Merton's vast literary legacy which summons the prayerful heart into rich and varied moods. *Versicles* and *antiphons* call us to prayer, *hymns* to lyricism of spirit attuning us to the unfolding of an earth day; *psalms* open us to intimate spiritual dialogue, *canticles* to praise, *litanies* to a dynamic spell of insight. We are offered *readings* and *responsories* for our deeper *lectio divina*, and *epistles* and *lessons* in Merton's voice to offer counsel and solid spiritual teaching, summarized in the form of a *collect*. We are challenged by his *exhortations*, and draw upon his *meditations* as inspiration for our own. The ancient practice of *examen* challenges us to intentionally witness the state and quality of our consciousness and conscience, and supports mindfulness about those habits of mind and heart that distort or enhance our true self. In the light of this deepening self-knowledge we make our *kyrie*, imploring mercy for our failings, grace for our spiritual authenticity.

When we are summoned to *silence*, we abandon thinking, letting ourselves sink like a stone to the bottom of a fathomless inner sea. In these quiet depths we begin to sense waves of wordless, quiet praise lapping against our hearts, entraining us to rhythms of a peace that is not conditional on the events of our lives, but on the quality of our deepening communion with God as we keep our daily appointments with mystery. In *intercessions* we raise up all those in need and our own intimate desires, remembering especially Merton's passionate intercession for peace on this earth. All this is gathered into the prayer Jesus taught us—a daily prayer for daily grace. Then Merton, faithful Abba of the virtual community of contemplative souls who pray his office, offers the master's *benediction*. Throughout the day we can sustain our contemplative mindfulness by constantly turning over the "chronic *koan*" or *breath prayer* that opens each hour. This practice of silently sounding a mantra can become a skillful means to remain anchored in contemplative awareness as we move from one thing to another. Above all we are encouraged to go slowly, breathe deeply, and let ourselves rest in the One funding each breath and sounding in every heartbeat.

Caveat lector: Some passages have been excerpted from the original text. In order to maintain a clean presentation for this Book of Hours, rather than note gaps with the customary ellipsis, we have instead highlighted these passages in the Notes with the notation *excerpted*. In all cases the original meaning has been diligently preserved.

These prayers, poems, and psalms are written in Merton's unique voice, the expression of his own intimate prayer, most composed between 1940 and 1968, before inclusive language was common practice. Since it is the commitment of the Merton Legacy Trust to protect the integrity of the Merton corpus, no alterations have been made to his voice.

SUNDAY

Dawn

* *

I only have time for eternity.

Opening Verse

raises and canticles anticipate
Each day the singing bells that wake the sun.
Open the secret eye of faith
And drink these deeps of invisible light.

Hymn

When psalms surprise me with their music
And antiphons turn to rum
The Spirit sings: the bottom drops out of my soul

And from the center of my cellar, Love,
    louder than thunder
Opens a heaven of naked air.

New eyes awaken.

I send Love's name into the world with wings
And songs grow up around me like a jungle.

Choirs of all creatures sing the tunes
Your Spirit played in Eden.

Zebras and antelopes and birds of paradise
Shine on the face of the abyss
And I am drunk with the great wilderness
Of the sixth day in Genesis.

Αντίρηοη

The most wonderful moment of the day is that when creation in its innocence asks permission to "be" once again, as it did on the first morning that ever was.

Ψαλμ

The first chirps of the waking birds mark the *"point vierge"*
    of the dawn
under a sky as yet without real light,
a moment of awe and inexpressible innocence,
when the Father in perfect silence opens their eyes.
They speak to Him, not with fluent song,
    but with an awakening question
that is their dawn state,
their state at the *"point vierge."*

Their condition asks if it is time for them to "be"?
He answers "Yes."

Then they one by one wake up, and become birds.
They manifest themselves as birds, beginning to sing.
Presently they will be fully themselves, and will even fly.

Meanwhile, the most wonderful moment of the day is that
when creation in its innocence asks permission
    to "be" once again,
as it did on the first morning that ever was.

All wisdom seeks to collect and manifest itself
    at that blind sweet point.
Man's wisdom does not succeed,
for we have fallen into self mastery and cannot ask
    permission of anyone.
We face our mornings as men of undaunted purpose.
We know the time and we dictate the terms.
We know what time it is.

For the birds there is not a time that they tell,
but the virgin point between darkness and light,
Between nonbeing and being.

So they wake: first the catbirds and cardinals.
Later the song sparrows and the wrens.
Last of all the doves and the crows.

Here is an unspeakable secret: paradise is all around us
    and we do not understand.
It is wide open. The sword is taken away,
    but we do not know it:
we are off "one to his farm and another
    to his merchandise."
Lights on. Clocks ticking. Thermostats working. Stoves
    cooking. Electric shavers filling radios with static.

"Wisdom," cries the dawn deacon, but we do not attend.

Antíphon

There are drops of dew that show like sapphires in the grass
as soon as the morning sun appears, and leaves stir behind
the hushed flight of an escaping dove.

Psalm

Today, Father, this blue sky lauds you.
The delicate green and orange flowers of the tulip poplar
    tree praise you.
The distant blue hills praise you, together with the
    sweet-smelling air that is full of brilliant light.
The bickering flycatchers praise you
with the lowing cattle and the quails that whistle over there.
I too, Father, praise you, with all these my brothers,
and they give voice to my own heart and to my own silence.
We are all one silence, and a diversity of voices.

You have made us together,
you have made us one and many,
you have placed me here in the midst as witness,
    as awareness, and as joy.

Here I am.

In me the world is present, and you are present.
I am a link in the chain of light and of presence.

You have made me a kind of center, but a center
    that is nowhere.
And yet also I am "here."

To be here with the silence of Sonship in my heart
is to be a center in which all things converge upon you.
That is surely enough for the time being.

PSALM PRAYER

I beg you to keep me in this silence so that I may learn
     from it
the word of your peace
and the word of your mercy
and the word of your gentleness to the world:
and that through me perhaps your word of peace
     may make itself heard
where it has not been possible for anyone to hear it
     for a long time.

READING

Contemplation is the response to a call: a call from Him
Who has no voice, and yet Who speaks in everything that is,
and Who, most of all, speaks in the depths of our own
being: for we ourselves are words of His. But we are words
that are meant to respond to Him, to answer to Him, to echo
Him, and even in some way to contain Him and signify Him.
Contemplation is this echo. It is a deep resonance in the
inmost center of our spirit in which our very life loses its
separate voice and re-sounds with the majesty and the mercy
of the Hidden and Living One. He answers Himself in us and
this answer is divine life, divine creativity, making all things
new. We ourselves become His echo and His answer. It is as if
in creating us God asked a question, and in awakening

us to contemplation He answered the question, so that the contemplative is at the same time, question and answer.

And all is summed up in one awareness—not a proposition, but an experience: "I Am."

SILENCE

RESPONSORY

The things of Time are in connivance with eternity.

CANTICLE

See the high birds! Is theirs the song
That flies among the wood-light
Wounding the listener with such bright arrows?

More than a season will be born here, nature,
In your world of gravid mirrors!
The quiet air awaits one note,
One light, one ray and it will be the angels' spring:
One flash, one glance upon the shiny pond, and then
Asperges me! sweet wilderness, and lo! we are redeemed!

For, like a grain of fire
Smouldering in the heart of every living essence
God plants His undivided power—
Buries His thought too vast for worlds
In seed and root and blade and flower,

Until, in the amazing shadowlights
Surcharging the religious silence of the spring

Creation finds the pressure of its everlasting secret
Too terrible to bear.

Then every way we look, lo! rocks and trees
Pastures and hills and streams and birds and firmament
And our own souls within us flash,
        and shower us with light,
While the wild countryside, unknown, unvisited
Bears sheaves of clean, transforming fire.

And then, oh then the written image, schooled in sacrifice,
The deep united threeness printed in our deepest being,
Shot by the brilliant syllable of such an intuition,
        turns within,
And plants that light far down into the heart of darkness
        and oblivion
And plunges after to discover flame.

Intercessions

The Lord's Prayer

Closing Prayer

With my hair almost on end and the eyes of the soul wide
        open I am present,
without knowing it at all, in this unspeakable Paradise,
        and I behold this secret,
this wide open secret which is there for everyone, free,
        and no one pays any attention.

O paradise of simplicity, self-awareness—
        and self-forgetfulness—liberty, peace.

DAY

· ·

Time, the Epiphany of the Creator,
the "Lord of Ages."

Exhortation

This is a country whose center is everywhere
and whose circumference is nowhere.
You do not find it by traveling but by standing
still.
Yet it is in this loneliness that the deepest
  activities begin.
It is here that you discover act without motion,
labor that is profound repose,
vision in obscurity,
and, beyond all desire,
a fulfillment whose limits extend to infinity.

It is a glorious destiny to be a member of the human race, though it is a race dedicated to many absurdities and one which makes many terrible mistakes: yet, with all that, God Himself gloried in becoming a member of the human race. A member of the human race! To think that such a commonplace realization should suddenly seem like news that one holds the winning ticket in a cosmic sweepstake.

I have the immense joy of being a member of a race in which God became incarnate. As if the sorrows and stupidities of the human condition could overwhelm me, now I realize what we all are. And if only everybody could realize this! But it cannot be explained. There is no way of telling people that they are all walking around shining like the sun.

It was as if I suddenly saw the secret beauty of their hearts, the depths of their hearts where neither sin nor desire nor self-knowledge can reach, the core of their reality, the person that each one is in God's eyes. If only they could all see themselves as they really are. If only we could see each other that way all the time. There would be no more war, no more hatred, no more cruelty, no more greed. I suppose the big problem would be that we would fall down and worship each other. But this cannot be seen, only believed and "understood" by a peculiar gift.

The fire of love for souls loved by God consumes like the fire of God's love, and it is the same love. It burns you up with a hunger for the supernatural happiness first of the people that you know, then of people you have barely heard of, and finally of everybody.

LESSON

This fire consumes you with a desire that is not directed immediately to action but to God. And in the swift, peaceful burning tide of that desire you are carried to prayer rather than to action, or rather, action seems to follow along with prayer and with desire, as if of its own accord.

You do not think much of what you are to do for souls: you are carried away to God by hunger and desire. And this hunger is exactly the same as the hunger for your own personal union with God, but now it includes someone else, and it is for God's own sake above all, though you do not reason and separate.

In this hunger there is pain and emptiness and there is joy and it is irresistible, and somehow it is full of the strong assurance that God wants to hear all your prayers.

Sometimes you get the feeling that, when you are carried away by this desire of love for souls, God is beginning to pour out everything upon you, to deluge you with all that you need, to overwhelm you with spiritual or even temporal favors, because you are no longer paying attention to your own needs, but are absorbed in the torment of desire for the happiness: of that soul—that soul—or that other one. Always individual and concrete.

It does not always have to be that way. You can lose sight of them all in God and pray for them as well or better perhaps, but it is still a sweet thing to be swept with the flames of this hunger and thirst for souls and, with a strange, mysterious sense of power, to obtain tremendous riches of joy for them from God.

It makes you want to sing, and songs come up from your heart and half smother you with joy. At the same time there is anguish as if your heart would burst, giving birth to the whole world.

COLLECT

The most important, the most real, and lasting work of the Christian is accomplished in the depths of his own soul.
It cannot be seen by anyone, even by himself.
It is known only to God.

EXAMEN

In a Zen koan someone said that an enlightened man is not one who seeks Buddha or finds Buddha, but simply an ordinary man who has nothing left to do. Yet stopping is not arriving. To stop is to stay a million miles from it and to do nothing is to miss it by the whole width of the universe.

As for arriving, when you arrive you are ruined. Yet how close the solution is: how simple it would be to have nothing more to do if only—one had really nothing more to do.

The man who is unripe cannot get there, no matter what he does or does not do. But the ripe fruit falls out of the tree without even thinking about it.

Why?

The man who is ripe discovers that there was never anything to be done from the very beginning.

Kyrie

Keep me, above all things, from sin.
But give me the strength that waits upon you in silence and
    peace.

Give me humility in which alone is rest,
and deliver me from pride which is the heaviest of burdens.

And possess my whole heart with the simplicity of love.
Occupy my whole life with the one thought and the one
    desire of love,
that I may love for You alone.

Benediction

We have a vocation not to be disturbed by the turmoil and
    wreckage of the great fabric of illusions.
Naturally we must suffer and feel to some extent
    lost in the tempest,
for we cannot be complacently "out" of it.

And yet we are, because of Him who dwells in us.

But precisely in Him and by Him we are deeply
    involved by compassion:
yet compassion is useless without freedom.

I am sure our desire to understand this paradox
    and live in fidelity to it
is the best indication that we can have the grace do so.

But none of it will come from our (outward) selves.

Dusk

....

*Eternity is in the present. Eternity is in
the palm of the hand.*

Opening Verse

 h pour your darkness and your brightness
over all our solemn valleys,
You skies: and travel like the gentle Virgin,
Toward the planets' stately setting.

Evening Hymn

My soul, O God, from Your fountains fill my will with fire.
Shine on my mind, "be darkness to my experience,"
occupy my heart with your tremendous Life.
Let my eyes see nothing in the world but Your glory,
and let my hands touch nothing that is not for Your service.
Let my tongue taste no bread that does not strengthen me
    to praise Your great mercy.
I will hear Your voice and I will hear all harmonies You
    have created,
singing Your hymns to find joy in giving You glory.

Aпτiρнoп

Go out from yourself with all that one is, which is nothing,
and pour out that nothingness in gratitude that God is who
He is.

Psaℓm

The Lord plays and diverts Himself in the garden
    of His creation,
and if we could let go of our own obsession
with what we think is the meaning of it all,
we might be able to hear His call
and follow Him in His mysterious, cosmic dance.

For the world and time are the dance of the Lord
    in emptiness.
The silence of the spheres is the music of a wedding feast.

The more we persist in misunderstanding
    the phenomena of life,
the more we analyze them out into strange finalities
and complex purposes of our own,
the more we involve ourselves in sadness, absurdity
    and despair.

But it does not matter much,
because no despair of ours can alter the reality of things,
or stain the joy of the cosmic dance which is always there.

Indeed we are in the midst of it, and it is in the midst of us,
for it beats in our very blood, whether we want it to or not.

Yet the fact remains that we are invited to forget ourselves
    on purpose,
cast our awful solemnity to the winds and join in
    the general dance.

Psalm Prayer

O perfect Word!
Whose Name is: "Savior,"
Whom we desire to hold;
Burn in our hearts, burn in our living marrow,
    own our being,
Hide us and heal us in the hug of Thy delight,
Whose admirable might
Sings in the furnace of the Triple Glory!

Epistle

It is not easy to try to say what I know I cannot say.
I do really have the feeling that you have seen something
most precious—and most available too. The reality that is
present to us and in us: call it Being, call it *Atman*, call it
Pneuma . . . or Silence.
And the simple fact that by being attentive, by learning to
listen
(or recovering the natural capacity to listen which cannot be
learned any more than breathing),
we can find ourself engulfed in such happiness that it cannot
be explained:
the happiness of being at one with everything in that hidden
ground of Love for which there can be no explanations.

I suppose what makes me most glad is that we all recognize each other in this metaphysical space of silence and happiness, and get some sense, for a moment, that we are full of paradise without knowing it.

Well, this is an attempt at answering all of you and saying that I am so happy that you enjoyed reading things I had written. May we all grow in grace and peace, and not neglect the silence that is printed in the center of our being.
It will not fail us. It is more than silence.
Jesus spoke of the spring of living water, you remember.

Silence

Responsory

Her love shapes worlds, shapes history, forms an Apocalypse in me and around me:
gives birth to the City of God.

Marian Canticle

Go, roads, to the four quarters of our quiet distance,
While you, full moon, wise queen,
Begin your evening journey to the hills of heaven,
And travel no less stately in the summer sky
Than Mary, going to the house of Zachary.

The woods are silent with the sleep of doves,
The valleys with the sleep of streams,
And all our barns are happy with peace of cattle
    gone to rest.

Still wakeful, in the fields, the shocks of wheat
Preach and say prayers:
You sheaves, make all your evensongs as sweet as ours,
Whose summer world, all ready for the granary and barn,
Seems to have seen, this day,
Into the secret of the Lord's Nativity.

Now at the fall of night, you shocks
Still bend your heads like kind and humble kings
The way you did this golden morning when you saw
        God's Mother passing,
While all our windows fill and sweeten
With the mild vespers of the hay and barley.

You moon and rising stars, pour on our barns and houses
Your gentle benedictions.
Remind us how our Mother, with far subtler
        and more holy influence,
Blesses our rooves and eaves,
Our shutters, lattices and sills,
Our doors, and floors, and stairs, and rooms,
        and bedrooms,
Smiling by night upon her sleeping children:
O gentle Mary! Our lovely Mother in heaven!

Intercessions

Almighty and merciful God, Father of all, Creator and
Ruler of the Universe, Lord of History, whose designs are
inscrutable, whose glory is without blemish, whose compassion for the errors of men is inexhaustible, in your will is
our peace.

In this fatal moment of choice in which we might begin
    the patient architecture of peace
We may also take the last step across the rim of chaos.
Save us then from our obsessions! Open our eyes,
    dissipate confusions,
Teach us to understand ourselves and our adversary!

Grant us to seek peace where it is truly found!
In your will, O God, is our peace!

Closing Prayer

This is the land where you have given me roots in eternity,
O God of heaven and earth.
This is the burning promised land, the house of God,
    the gate of heaven,
the place of peace,
the place of silence,
the place of wrestling with the angel.

Dark

*The world and time are the dance of
the Lord in emptiness.*

Opening Verse

 night of admiration, full of choirs,
O night of deepest praise,
And darkness full of sweet delight!
What secret and intrepid Visitor
Has come to raise us from the dead?
He softly springs the locks of time, our sepulchre,
In the foretold encounter.

Night Hymn

City, when we see you coming down,
Coming down from God
To be the new world's crown:
How shall they sing, the fresh, unsalted seas
Hearing your harmonies!

For there is no more death,
No need to cure those waters, now, with any brine;
Their shores give them no dead,
Rivers no blood, no rot to stain them.
Because the cruel algebra of war
Is now no more.
And the steel circle of time, inexorable,
Bites like a padlock shut, forever,
In the smoke of the last bomb:
And in that trap the murderers and sorcerers
    and crooked leaders
Go rolling home to hell.
And history is done.

Shine with your lamb-light, shine upon the world:
You are the new creation's sun.
And standing on their twelve foundations,
Lo, the twelve gates that are One Christ are wide as canticles:
And Oh I Begin to hear the thunder of the songs
    within the crystal Towers,
While all the saints rise from their earth with feet like light
And fly to tread the quick-gold of those streets,

Oh City, when we see you sailing down,
Sailing down from God,
Dressed in the glory of the Trinity, and angel-crowned
In nine white diadems of liturgy.

Αntiphon

The low walls of the western world are burning down,
The woods go up to meet
The white battalions of the rising night.

Psalm

There is no where in you a paradise that is no place
    and there
You do not enter except without a story.
To enter there is to become unnameable.

Whoever is there is homeless for he has no door
    and no identity
with which to go out and to come in.

Whoever is nowhere is nobody, and therefore cannot exist
    except as unborn:
No disguise will avail him anything

Such a one is neither lost nor found.

But he who has an address is lost.

They fall, they fall into apartments and are
    securely established!

They find themselves in streets. They are licensed
To proceed from place to place
They now know their own names
They can name several friends and know
Their own telephones must some time ring.

If all telephones ring at once, if all names are shouted at
    once and
all cars crash at one crossing:
If all cities explode and fly away in dust
Yet identities refuse to be lost. There is a name and number
    for everyone.

There is a definite place for bodies, there are pigeon holes
    for ashes:
Such security can business buy!

Who would dare to go nameless in so secure a universe?
Yet, to tell the truth, only the nameless are at home in it.

They bear with them in the center of nowhere the unborn
    flower of nothing:
This is the paradise tree. It must remain unseen until words
    end and arguments are silent.

PSALM PRAYER

I entered into the everlasting movement of that gravitation
which is the very life and spirit of God: God's own gravitation towards the depths of his own infinite nature, his goodness without end. And God, that center who is everywhere,
and whose circumference is nowhere, finding me, through
incorporation with Christ, incorporated into this immense
and tremendous gravitational movement which is love,
which is the Holy Spirit, loved me.

And he called out to me from his own immense depths.

SILENCE

Litany

Teach me to go to this country beyond words and beyond names.

Teach me to pray on this side of the frontier, here where these woods are.

I need to be led by you.

I need my heart to be moved by you.

I need my soul to be made clean by your prayer.

I need my will to be made strong by you.

I need the world to be saved and changed by you.

I need you for all those who suffer, who are in prison, in danger, in sorrow.

I need you for all the crazy people.

I need your healing hand to work always in my life.

I need you to make me, as you made your Son, a healer, a comforter, a savior.

I need you to name the dead.

I need you to help the dying cross their particular rivers.

I need you for myself whether I live or die.

It is necessary. Amen.

Closing Prayer

You, Who sleep in my breast, are not met with words, but in the emergence of life within life and of wisdom within wisdom. You are found in communion: Thou in me and I in Thee and Thou in them and they in me: dispossession within dispossession, dispassion within dispassion, emptiness within emptiness, freedom within freedom. I am alone. Thou art alone. The Father and I are One.

MONDAY

Dawn

It is morning, afternoon or evening.
Begin.

Opening Verse

weet Christ, discover diamonds
And sapphires in my verse
While I burn the sap of my pine house
For the praise of the ocean sun.

Hymn

A yellow flower
(Light and spirit)
Sings by itself
For nobody.

A golden spirit
(Light and emptiness)
Sings without a word
By itself.

Let no one touch this gentle sun
In whose dark eye
Someone is awake.

(No light, no gold, no name, no color
And no thought:
O, wide awake!)

A golden heaven
Sings by itself
A song to nobody.

Αντιρηον

My worship is a blue sky and ten thousand crickets in the deep wet hay of the field. My vow is the silence under their song.

Psalm

The forms and individual characters of living
    and growing things,
of inanimate beings, of animals and flowers and all nature,
constitute their holiness in the sight of God.

Their inscape is their sanctity.
It is the imprint of His wisdom and His reality in them.
The special clumsy beauty of this particular
colt on this day in this field under these clouds
is a holiness consecrated to God by His own
    creative wisdom
and it declares the glory of God.

The pale flowers of the dogwood outside this window
     are saints.
The little yellow flowers that nobody notices on the edge of
     that road are saints
looking up into the face of God.

This leaf has its own texture and its own pattern of veins
     and its own holy shape,
and the bass and trout hiding in the deep pools of the river
are canonized by their beauty and their strength.

The lakes hidden among the hills are saints,
and the sea too is a saint who praises God
     without interruption
in her majestic dance.

The great, gashed, half-naked mountain is another
     of God's saints.
There is no other like him.
He is alone in his own character;
nothing else in the world ever did or ever will imitate God
     in quite the same way.
That is his sanctity.

But what about you? What about me?

Psalm Prayer

We are warmed by fire, not by the smoke of the fire.
We are carried over the sea by a ship, not by the wake
     of a ship.
So too, what we are is to be sought in the invisible depths
     of our own being,
not in our outward reflection in our own acts.

Reading

When I speak of the contemplative life I do not mean the institutional cloistered life, the organized life of prayer. I am talking about a special dimension of inner discipline and experience, a certain integrity and fullness of personal development, which are not compatible with a purely external, alienated, busy-busy existence. This does not mean that they are incompatible with action, with creative work, with dedicated love. On the contrary, these all go together. A certain depth of disciplined experience is a necessary ground for fruitful action. Without a more profound human understanding derived from exploration of the inner ground of human existence, love will tend to be superficial and deceptive. Traditionally, the ideas of prayer, meditation and contemplation have been associated with this deepening of one's personal life and this expansion of the capacity to understand and serve others.

Silence

Responsory

Sink from your shallows, soul, into eternity.
We touch the rays we cannot see.
We feel the light that seems to sing.

Canticle

We have found the places where the Lord of Songs,
where the Nameless lies down in groves

making his light too shy. The valley flowers
with him. He sleeps in the sacred meadow,
he wakes in rain on the secular hill.
We have found him to be neither one nor the other,
neither sacred nor secular.

We have found places where the Lord of Songs
visits his beloved. Crossroads. Hilltops. Market towns.
Ball courts. Harbors. Crossroads. Meeting places.
Bridges. Places where the Lord of Songs
is refreshed. Crossroads.
It is when the Stranger is met and know
at the unplanned crossing
that the Nameless becomes a Name.

Intercessions

The Lord's Prayer

Closing Prayer

Let us live in this love and this happiness, you and I and all
of us, in the love of Christ and in contemplation, for this is
where we find ourselves and one another as we truly are. It is
only in this love that we at last become real. For it is here
that we most truly share the life of One God in Three
Persons.

DAY

All Christian life is meant to be at the same time profoundly contemplative and rich in active work.

Exhortation

hristian holiness can no longer be considered a matter purely of individual and isolated acts of virtue. It must also be seen as part of a great collaborative effort for spiritual and cultural renewal in society, to produce conditions in which all can work and enjoy the just fruits of their labor in peace.

Meditation

The requirements of a work to be done can be understood as the will of God. If I am supposed to hoe a garden or make a table, then I will be obeying God if I am true to the task I am performing. To do the work carefully and well, with love and respect for the nature of my task and with due attention to its purpose, is to unite myself to God's will in my work. In this way I become His instrument. He works through me. When I act as His instrument my labor cannot become an obstacle to contemplation. Yet my work itself will purify and pacify my mind and dispose me for contemplation.

Unnatural, frantic, anxious work, work done under pressure of greed or fear or any other inordinate passion, cannot properly speaking be dedicated to God, because God never wills such work directly.

He may permit that through no fault of our own we may have to work madly and distractedly, due to our sins and to the sins of the society in which we live. In that case we must tolerate it and make the best of what we cannot avoid. But let us not be blind to the distinction between sound, healthy work and unnatural toil.

Prayer

My only desire is to give myself completely to the action of this infinite love Who is God, Who demands to transform me into Himself secretly, darkly, in simplicity, in a way that has no drama about it and is infinitely beyond everything spectacular and astonishing, so is its significance and its power.

LESSON

Keep your eyes clean and your ears quiet and your mind serene. Breathe God's air.

Work, if you can, under His sky.

But if you have to live in a city and work among machines and ride in the subways and eat in a place where the radio makes you deaf with spurious news and where the food destroys your life and the sentiments of those around you poison your heart with boredom, do not be impatient, but accept it as the love of God and as a seed of solitude planted in your soul.

If you are appalled by those things, you will keep your appetite for the healing silence of recollection. But meanwhile— keep your sense of compassion for the men who have forgotten the very concept of solitude.

You, at least, know that it exists, and that it is the source of peace and joy.

You can still hope for such joy. They do not even hope for it any more.

COLLECT

Beloved Spirit, You are all the prudence and the power
That change our dust and nothing into fields and fruits;
Enfold our lives forever in the compass
    of Your peaceful hills.

Examen

Perhaps I am stronger than I think.
Perhaps I am even afraid of my strength, and turn it against
    myself, thus making myself weak.
Making myself secure. Making myself guilty.
Perhaps I am most afraid of the strength of God in me.
Perhaps I would rather be guilty and weak in myself,
than strong in Him whom I cannot understand.

Kyrie

Keep me, above all things, from sin.

Keep me from the death of deadly sin
    which puts hell in my soul.
Keep me from the murder of lust
    that binds and poisons my heart.
Keep me from the sins that eat flesh with irresistible fire.

And then to wait in peace and emptiness and oblivion
    of all things.

Benediction

And lo! God my God!
Look! Look! I travel in Thy strength
I swing in the grasp of Thy Love, Thy great Love's
    One Strength,
I run Thy swift ways, Thy straightest rails
Until my life become Thy Life and sails or rides
    like an express!

Dusk

I thank God for the present.

hrist the High Priest is awakening in the depths
of my soul
in silence and majesty, like a giant Who means
to run His course.

Evening Hymn

Minds, minds, sing like spring
To see the hills that fling their hands into the air:
To see the trees all yield their gladness to the tender winds
And open wide their treasuries:
Behold the birds, released like angels,
    from those leafy palaces,
With fire and blue and red-gold splashing
    in their painted wings,
Each one proclaiming part of the Apocalypse.
They aim their flights at all the four horizons
And fire their arrows of tremendous news.

World, world, sing like spring
To hear the harvests praising
Heaven with a thousand voices:
Behold the fertile clouds, in golden fleets,
Like flying frigates, full of gifts.
Behold the clouds, with loads of Gospel,
Splendid and simple as Apostles, in their outward flight!
The waters of the sea all flash with laughter,
Leaping as if to kiss those high, high galleons,
That ride the heavens, full of freight.

But who shall tell the blazes and exchanges
The hidden lightning and the smiles of blinding night,
The kiss and vanish of the sudden invitation,
The game and promise of espousal?

O Holy Spirit, hear, we call Your Name aloud,
We speak You plain and humble in the terms of prayer,
Whatever talk You grant us.

Antiphon

I no longer want to have anything to do with love that
forgets to be grateful.
Otherwise I will only go on lying to You:
and I want to be done with all insincerity for ever and for
ever.

Psalm

It is God's love that warms me in the sun
and God's love that sends the cold rain.

It is God's love that feeds me in the bread I eat
and God that feeds me also by hunger and fasting.
It is the love of God that sends the winter days
    when I am cold and sick,
and the hot summer when I labor and my clothes are
    full of sweat:
but it is God Who breathes on me with light winds off
the river and in the breezes out of the wood.
His love spreads the shade of the sycamore over my head.

It is God's love that speaks to me in the birds and streams;
but also behind the clamor of the city God speaks to me
    in His judgments,
and all these things are seeds sent to me from His will.

If these seeds would take root in my liberty,
and if His will would grow from my freedom,
I would become the love that He is,
and my harvest would be His glory and my own joy.

And I would grow together with thousands and millions
    of other freedoms
into the gold of one huge field praising God,
loaded with increase, loaded with wheat.

Psalm Prayer

From moment to moment I remember with astonishment
that I am at the same time empty and full, and satisfied
(because I am empty. I lack nothing. The Lord rules me).

Epistle

All Christian life is meant to be at the same time profoundly contemplative and rich in active work. It is true that we are called to create a better world. But we are first of all called to a more immediate and exalted task: that of creating our own lives. In doing this, we act as co-workers with God. We take our place in the great work of mankind, since in effect the creation of our own destiny, in God, is impossible in pure isolation. Each one of us works out his own destiny in inseparable union with all those others with whom God has willed us to live. We share with one another the creative work of living in the world. And it is through our struggle with material reality, with nature, that we help one another create at the same time our own destiny and a new world for our descendants.

Silence

Responsory

Lady, Queen of Heaven, pray me into solitude and silence and unity, that all my ways may be immaculate in God. Let me be content with whatever darkness surrounds me, finding Him always by me, in His mercy.

Marian Canticle

Why do you fly from the drowned shores of Galilee,
From the sands and the lavender water?
Why do you leave the ordinary world, Virgin of Nazareth,

The yellow fishing boats, the farms,
The winesmelling yards and low cellars
Or the oilpress, and the women by the well?
Why do you fly those markets,
Those suburban gardens,
The trumpets of the jealous lilies,
Leaving them all, lovely among the lemon trees?

You have trusted no town
With the news behind your eyes
You have drowned Gabriel's word in thoughts like seas
And turned toward the stone mountain
To the treeless places.
Virgin of God, why are your clothes like sails?

The day Our Lady, full of Christ,
Entered the dooryard of her relative
Did not her steps, light steps, lay on the paving leaves like
    gold?
Did not her eyes as grey as doves
Alight like the peace of a new world upon that house, upon
    miraculous Elizabeth?

Her salutation
Sings in the stone valley like a Charterhouse bell:
And the unborn saint John
Wakes in his mother's body,
Bounds with the echoes of discovery.

Intercessions

Almighty and merciful God, Father of all, Creator and
Ruler of the Universe, Lord of History, whose designs are

inscrutable, whose glory is without blemish, whose compassion for the errors of men is inexhaustible, in your will is our peace.

> Help us to be masters of the weapons that threaten to master us.
> Help us to use our science for peace and plenty, not for war and destruction.
> Show us how to use atomic power to bless our children's children, not to blight them.

Grant us to seek peace where it is truly found!
In your will, O God, is our peace!

The Lord's Prayer

Closing Prayer

Our glory and our hope—We are the Body of Christ. Christ loves us and espouses us as His own flesh. Isn't that enough for us? But we do not really believe it. No!

Be content, be content. We are the Body of Christ. We have found Him, He has found us. We are in Him, He is in us. There is nothing further to look for, except for the deepening of this life we already possess. Be content.

DARK

God cannot be found by weighing the present against the future or the past, but only by sinking into the heart of the present as it is.

OPENING VERSE

ay my bones burn and ravens eat my flesh
If I forget thee, contemplation!
May language perish from my tongue
If I do not remember thee, O Sion, city of vision,
Whose heights have windows finer than the firmament
When night pours down her canticles
And peace sings on thy watchtowers like the stars of Job.

NIGHT HYMN

In my ending is my meaning
Says the season.

No clock:
Only the heart's blood
Only the word.

O lamp
Weak friend
In the knowing night!

O tongue of flame
Under the heart
Speak softly:
For love is black
Says the season.

Midnight!
Kissed with flame!
See! See!
My love is darkness!

Only in the Void
Are all ways one:

Only in the night
Are all the lost
Found.

In my ending is my meaning.

Αntίρηοη

Here is liberty, all I have to do is to be quiet, sit still.

Night Psalm

Be still
Listen to the stones of the wall.
Be silent, they try
To speak your

Name.
Listen
To the living walls.
Who are you?
Who
Are you? Whose
Silence are you?

Who (be quiet)
Are you (as these stones
Are quiet). Do not
Think of what you are
Still less of
What you may one day be.
Rather
Be what you are (but who?) be
The unthinkable one
You do not know.

O be still, while
You are still alive,
And all things live around you
Speaking (I do not hear)
To your own being,

Speaking by the Unknown
That is in you and in themselves.

"I will try, like them
To be my own silence:
And this is difficult. The whole
World is secretly on fire. The stones
Burn, even the stones
They burn me. How can a man be still or
Listen to all things burning? How can he dare
To sit with them when
All their silence
Is on fire?"

Psalm Prayer

Take thought tonight. Take thought tonight when it is dark, when it is raining. Take thought of the game you have forgotten. You are the child of a great and peaceful race, an unutterable fable. You were discovered on a mild mountain. You have come up out of the godlike ocean. You are holy, disarmed, signed with a chaste emblem. You are also marked with forgetfulness. Deep inside your breast you wear the number of loss. Take thought tonight. Do this. Do this. Recover your original name.

Silence

Litany

No matter how simple discourse may be,
    it is never simple enough.
No matter how simple thought may be,
    it is never simple enough.
No matter how simple love may be,
    it is never simple enough.
The only thing left is the simplicity of the soul in God,
or better, the simplicity of God.

Closing Prayer

"O the depth of the riches of the wisdom and knowledge of God!"

A door opens in the center of our being and we seem to fall through it into immense depths which, although they are infinite, are all accessible to us; all eternity seems to have become ours in this one placid and breathless contact.

† TUESDAY

Dawn

∙∙

*Prayer belongs less to time than to
eternity.*

Opening Verse

he birds begin to wake.
It will soon be dawn.
In an hour or two the towns will wake, and
men will enjoy everywhere
the great luminous smiles of production and
business.

Hymn

How long we wait, with minds as quiet as time,
Like sentries on a tower.
How long we watch, by night, like the astronomers.

Heaven, when will we hear you sing,
Arising from our grassy hills,

And say: "The dark is done, and Day
Laughs like a Bridegroom in His tent, the lovely sun,
His tent the sun, His tent the smiling sky!"

How long we wait with minds as dim as ponds
While stars swim slowly homeward in the water of our
    west!
Heaven, when will we hear you sing?

How long we listened to the silence of our vineyards
And heard no bird stir in the rising barley.
The stars go home behind the shaggy trees.
Our minds are grey as rivers.
O earth, when will you wake in the green wheat,
And all our cedars sing:
"Bright land, lift up your leafy gates!
You abbey steeple, sing with bells!
For look, our Sun rejoices like a dancer
On the rim of our hills."

In the blue west the moon is uttered like the word:
    "Farewell."

Αντιρhon

Morning, lean into new light.
Listen to well-ordered hills go by, rank upon rank,
    in the sun.
The sound of the earth goes up to embrace
    the constant sky.
My own center is the teeming heart of natural families.

Psalm

When no one listens
To the quiet trees

When no one notices
The sun in the pool

Where no one feels
The first drop of rain
Or sees the last star

Or hails the first morning
Of a giant world
Where peace begins
And rages end:

One bird sits still
Watching the work of God:
One turning leaf,
Two falling blossoms,
Ten circles upon the pond.

One cloud upon the hillside,
Two shadows in the valley
And the light strikes home.

Now dawn commands the capture
Of the tallest fortune,
The surrender
Of no less marvelous prize!

Closer and clearer
Than any wordy master,
Thou inward Stranger
Whom I have never seen,

Deeper and cleaner
Than the clamorous ocean,

Seize up my silence
Hold me in Thy Hand!

Now act is waste
And suffering undone
Laws become prodigals
Limits are torn down
For envy has no property
And passion is none.

Look, the vast Light stands still
Our cleanest Light is One!

Psalm Prayer

I am under the sky. The birds are all silent. But the frogs have begun singing their pleasure in all the waters and in the warm, green places where the sunshine is wonderful. Praise Christ, all you living creatures. For Him you and I were created. With every breath we love Him. My psalms fulfill your dim, unconscious song, O brothers in this wood.

Reading

We are what we love. If we love God, in whose image we were created, we discover ourselves in him and we cannot help being happy: we have already achieved something of the fullness of being for which we were destined in our creation. If we love everything else but God, we contradict the image born in our very essence, and we cannot help being unhappy, because we are living a caricature of what we are meant to be.

Silence

Responsory

How long we wait, with minds as quiet as time.

Canticle

O paradise, O child's world!
Where all the grass lives
And all the animals are aware!
The huge sun, bigger than the house
Stands and streams with life in the east
While in the west a thunder cloud
Moves away forever.

No blade of grass is not blessed
On this archetypal, cosmic hill,
This womb of mysteries.

Intercessions

The Lord's Prayer

Closing Prayer

Let us then continue united in prayer and faith, and realize more and more the truth and mercy of God in our lives. For we are called above all to be signs of His mercy in the world, and our fidelity will in its turn be a small sign to others of His fidelity, not that our fidelity has any value of itself, but it enables Him to give us richer blessings and to manifest Himself in doing good to us who are nothing.

Day

I hear a machine, a bird, a clock.

Exhortation

L ife is not accomplishing some special work but attaining to a degree of consciousness and inner freedom which is beyond all works and attainments. That is my real goal. It implies "becoming unknown and as nothing."

Meditation

Lord, I have not lived like a contemplative. The first essential is missing. I only say I trust You. My actions prove that the one I trust is myself —and that I am still afraid of You.

Take my life into Your hands, at last, and do whatever You want with it. I give myself to Your love and mean to keep on giving myself to Your love—rejecting neither the hard things nor the pleasant things You have arranged for me. It is enough for me that You have glory. Everything You have planned is good. It is all love.

The way You have laid open before me is an easy way, compared with the hard way of my own will which leads back to Egypt, and to bricks without straw. If You allow people to praise me, I shall worry even less, but be glad. If You send me work I shall embrace it with joy and it will be rest to me, because it is Your will. And if You send me rest, I will rest in You.

Only save me from myself. Save me from my own, private, poisonous urge to change everything, to act without reason, to move for movement's sake, to unsettle everything You have ordained. Let me rest in Your will and be silent. Then the light of Your joy will warm my life. Its fire will burn in my heart and shine for Your glory. This is what I live for. Amen, amen.

PRAYER

My intention is to give myself entirely and without compromise to whatever work God wants to perform in me and through me.

LESSON

Our vocation is not simply to be, but to work together with God in the creation of our own life, our own identity, our own destiny. This means to say that we should not passively exist, but actively participate in His creative freedom, in our own lives, and in the lives of others, by choosing the truth.

To put it better, we are even called to share with God the work of creating the truth of our identity. We can evade this responsibility by playing with masks, and this pleases us because it can appear at times to be a free and creative way of living. It is quite easy, it seems, to please everyone. But in the long run the cost and the sorrow come very high. To work out our own identity in God, which the Bible calls "working out our salvation," is a labor that requires sacrifice and anguish, risk and many tears. It demands close attention to reality at every moment, and great fidelity to God as He reveals Himself, obscurely, in the mystery of each new situation.

We do not know clearly beforehand what the result of this work will be. The secret of my full identity is hidden in Him. He alone can make me who I am, or rather who I will be when at last I fully begin to be. But unless I desire this identity and work to find it with Him and in Him, the work will never be done. The way of doing it is a secret I can learn from no one else but Him. There is no way of attaining to the secret without faith. But contemplation is the greater and more precious gift, for it enables me to see and understand the work that He wants done.

Collect

The seeds that are planted in my liberty at every moment, by God's will, are the seeds of my own identity, my own reality, my own happiness, my own sanctity.

To refuse them is to refuse everything; it is the refusal of my own existence and being: of my identity, my very self.

Examen

I think what I need to learn is an almost infinite tolerance and compassion because negative thought gets nowhere. I am beginning to think that in our time we will correct almost nothing, and get almost nowhere: but if we can just prepare a compassionate and receptive soil for the future, we will have done a great work. I feel at least that this is the turn my own life ought to take.

Kyrie

Keep me, above all things, from sin.

Keep me from loving money in which is hatred,
From avarice and ambition that suffocate my life.

Keep me from the deadly works of vanity
and the thankless labor for pride and money
    and reputation.

Benediction

Be content that you are not yet a saint, even though you realize that the only thing worth living for is sanctity. Then you will be satisfied to let God lead you to sanctity by paths that you cannot understand. You will travel in darkness in which you will no longer be concerned with yourself and no longer compare yourself to other men. Those who have gone by that way have finally found out that sanctity is in everything and that God is all around them, they suddenly wake up and find that the joy of God is everywhere.

DUSK

··

The reality of now—the unreality of
all the rest.

OPENING VERSE

e lift our eyes to you in heaven, O God of
eternity, wishing we were poorer,
more silent, more mortified.
Lord, give us liberty from all the things that
are in this world,
from the preoccupations of earth and of time,
that we may be called to cleanness,
where the saints are, the gold and silver saints
  before your throne.

EVENING HYMN

Under the blunt pine
I who am not sent
Remain. The pathway dies,
The journey has begun.

Here the bird abides
And sings on top of the forgotten
Storm. The ground is warm.
He sings no particular message.
His hymn has one pattern, no more planned,
No less perfectly planned
And no more arbitrary
Than the pattern in the seed, the salt,
The snow, the cell, the drop of rain.

The free man is not alone as busy men are
But as birds are. The free man sings
Alone as universes do. Built
Upon his own inscrutable pattern
Clear, unmistakable, not invented by himself alone
Or for himself, but for the universe also.

Nor does he make it his business to be recognized
Or care to have himself found out
As if some special subterfuge were needed
To get himself known for who he is.
The free man does not float
On the tides of his own expedition
Nor is he sent on ventures as busy men are,
Bound to an inexorable result:
But like the birds or lilies
He seeks first the Kingdom, without care.
Nor need the free man remember
Any street or city, or keep campaigns
In his head, or countries for that matter
Or any other economy.

Under the blunt pine
Elias becomes his own geography
(Supposing geography to be necessary at all),
Elias becomes his own wild bird, with God in the center,
His own wide field which nobody owns,
His own pattern, surrounding the Spirit
By which he is himself surrounded:

For the free man's road has neither beginning nor end.

Antiphon

The great comfort is in the goodness and sweetness and
nearness of all God has made, and the created *isness* which
makes Him first of all present in us, speaking us.

Psalm

Let this be my only consolation—that, wherever I am,
You my Lord are loved and praised.
The trees indeed love You without knowing You.
Without being aware of Your presence,
the tiger lilies and cornflowers proclaim that they love You.
The beautiful dark clouds ride slowly across the sky
    musing on You
like children who do not know what they are dreaming of
    as they play.

In the midst of them all, I know You and I know
    of Your Presence.
In them and in me I know of the love that they do not
    know and,

what is greater, I am abashed by the presence of Your love
in me.
O kind and terrible love which You have given me
and which could never be in my heart if You did not
love me!

In the midst of these beings that have never offended You,
I am loved by You, most of all as one who has offended
You.
I am seen by You under the sky and my offenses have been
forgotten by You.

Psalm Prayer

You ask of me nothing else than to be content that I am
your Child and your Friend, simply to accept your friendship because it is your friendship. This friendship is Spirit.
You have called me to be repeatedly born in the Spirit,
repeatedly born in light, in knowledge, in unknowing, in
faith, in awareness, in gratitude, in poverty, in presence, and
in praise.

Epistle

Let us suppose the message of a so-called contemplative to a
so-called man of the world to be something like this:

My dear brother, can I tell you that I have found answers to
the questions that torment the man of our time?

I do not know if I have found answers. When I first became a
monk, yes, I was more sure of "answers." But as I grow old in
the monastic life and advance further into solitude, I become

aware that I have only begun to seek the questions. And what are the questions? Can man make sense out of his existence? Can man honestly give his life meaning merely by adopting a certain set of explanations which pretend to tell him why the world began and where it will end, why there is evil and what is necessary for a good life? My brother, perhaps in my solitude, I have become as it were an explorer for you, a searcher in realms which you are not able to visit—except perhaps in the company of your psychiatrist. I have been summoned to explore a desert area of man's heart in which explanations no longer suffice, and in which one learns that only experience counts. An arid, rocky, dark land of the soul, sometimes illuminated by strange fires which men fear and peopled by specters which men studiously avoid except in their nightmares. And in this area I have learned that one cannot truly know hope unless he has found out how like despair hope is. The language of Christianity has said this for centuries in other less naked terms.

Silence

Responsory

Glorious Mother of God, shall I ever again distrust you,
    or your God,
before whose throne you are irresistible
    in your intercession?

Shall I ever turn my eyes from your hands and from your
    face and from your eyes?
Shall I ever look anywhere else but in the face of your love,
to find out true counsel, and know my way,
in all the days and all the moments of my life?

Marian Canticle

Because my will's simple as a window
And knows no pride of original earth,
It is my life to die, like glass, by light:
Slain in the strong rays of the bridegroom sun.

Because my love is simple as a window
And knows no shame of original dust,

I longed all night, (when I was visible) for dawn my death:
When I would marry day, my Holy Spirit:
And die by transubstantiation into light.

For light, my lover, steals my life in secret.
I vanish into day, and leave no shadow
But the geometry of my cross,
Whose frame and structure are the strength
By which I die, but only to the earth,
And am uplifted to the sky my life.
When I become the substance of my lover,
(Being obedient, sinless glass)
I love all things that need my lover's life,
And live to give my newborn Morning to your quiet
    rooms,

Your rooms, that would be tombs,
Or vaults of night, and death, and terror,

Fill with the clarity of living Heaven,
Shine with the rays of God's Jerusalem:
O shine, bright Sions!

Because I die by brightness and the Holy Spirit,
The sun rejoices in your jail, my kneeling Christian,
(Where even now you weep and grin
To learn, from my simplicity, the strength of faith.)

Therefore do not be troubled at the judgments
    of the thunder.
Stay still and pray, still stay, my other son,
And do not fear the armies and black ramparts
Of the advancing and retreating rains:
I'll let no lightning kill your room's white order.

Although it is the day's last hour,
Look with no fear:
For the torn storm lets in, at the world's rim,
Three streaming rays as straight as Jacob's ladder:

And you shall see the sun, my Son, my Substance,
Come to convince the world of the day's end,
    and of the night,
Smile to the lovers of the day in smiles of blood:
For through my love, He'll be their Brother,
My light—the Lamb of their Apocalypse.

Intercessions

Almighty and merciful God, Father of all, Creator and
Ruler of the Universe, Lord of History, whose designs are
inscrutable, whose glory is without blemish, whose compassion

107

for the errors of men is inexhaustible, in your will is our peace.

Save us from the compulsion to follow our adversaries in all that we most hate, confirming them in their hatred and suspicion of us.

Resolve our inner contradictions, which now grow beyond belief and beyond bearing.

They are at once a torment and a blessing: for if you had not left us the light of conscience, we would not have to endure them.

Grant us to seek peace where it is truly found!

In your will, O God, is our peace!

†he Lord's Prayer

Closing Prayer

We must respond to God's gifts gladly and freely with thanksgiving, happiness and joy: but in contemplation we thank Him less by words than by the serene happiness of silent acceptance. "Be empty and see that I am God." It is our emptiness in the presence of the abyss of His reality, our silence in the presence of His infinitely rich silence, our joy in the bosom of the serene darkness in which His light holds us absorbed, it is all this that praises Him. It is this that causes love of God and wonder and adoration to swim up into us like tidal waves out of the depths of that peace, and break upon the shores of our consciousness in a vast, hushed surf of inarticulate praise, praise and glory!

DARK

. . . .

More nourishment and strength in
one hour of obscurity than in ten
weeks of thinking.

OPENING VERSE

ur lives, like candles, spell this simple symbol:
Weep like our bodily life, sweet work of bees,
Sweeten the world, with your slow sacrifice.
And this shall be our praise:
That by our glad expense, our Father's will
Burned and consumed us for a parable.

NIGHT HYMN

When in the soul of the serene disciple
With no more Fathers to imitate
Poverty is a success,
It is a small thing to say the roof is gone:
He has not even a house.

Stars, as well as friends,
Are angry with the noble ruin.
Saints depart in several directions.
Be still:
There is no longer any need of comment.

It was a lucky wind
That blew away his halo with his cares,
A lucky sea that drowned his reputation.

Here you will find
Neither a proverb nor a memorandum.
There are no ways,
No methods to admire
Where poverty is no achievement.
His God lives in his emptiness like an affliction.

What choice remains?
Well, to be ordinary is not a choice:
It is the usual freedom
Of men without visions.

Antiphon

Lord God of this great night:
Do You see that my soul is beginning to dissolve like wax
within me?

Night Psalm

Lord, receive my prayer
Sweet as incense smoke

Rising from my heart
Full of care
I lift up my hands
In evening sacrifice
Lord, receive my prayer.

I meet the man
On my way
When he starts to curse
And threatens me,
Lord, guard my lips
I will not reply
Guide my steps in the night
As I go my way.

Maybe he belongs
To some other Lord

Who is not so wise and good
Maybe that is why those bones
Lie scattered on his road.

When I look to right and left
No one cares to know
Who I am, where I go.

Hear my prayer
I will trust in you
If they set their traps
On my way
If they aim their guns at me
You will guide my steps
I will pass them by

III

In the dark
They will never see.
Lord, to you I raise
Wide and bright
Faith-filled eyes
In the night
You are my protection
Bring me home.

And receive my prayer
Sweet as incense smoke
Rising from my heart
Free of care.

PSALM PRAYER

If the salvation of society depends, in the long run, on the moral and spiritual health of individuals, the subject of contemplation becomes a vastly important one, since contemplation is one of the indications of spiritual maturity. It is closely allied to sanctity. You cannot save the world merely with a system. You cannot have peace without charity. You cannot have social order without saints, mystics, and prophets.

SILENCE

LITANY

My God, I want to love You.
I want my will to disappear in Your will.

I want to be one spirit with You.
I want to become all Your desires and thoughts.
I want to live in the middle of Your Trinity and praise You
with the flames of your own praise.

Closing Prayer

God touches us with a touch that is emptiness and empties
us. He moves us with a simplicity that simplifies us. All variety, all complexity, all paradox, all multiplicity cease. Our
mind swims in the air of an understanding, a reality that is
dark and serene and includes in itself everything. Nothing
more is desired. Nothing more is wanting. Our only sorrow,
if sorrow be possible at all, is the awareness that we ourselves still live outside of God.

WEDNESDAY

Dawn

What secret and intrepid Visitor
softly springs the locks of time?

Opening Verse

ur souls rise up from our earth like Jacob waking from his dream and exclaiming: "Truly God is in this place and I knew it not"! God becomes the only reality, in Whom all other reality takes its proper place—and falls into insignificance.

Hymn

O land alive with miracles!
O clad in streams
Lift your blue trees into the early sun!

O country wild with talent
Is there an hour in you that does not rouse our mind with
 songs?
The boughs that bend in the weak wind

Open us momentary windows, here and there,
Into those deep and purple galleries,
Disclosing us the birds your genius.

O brilliant wood!
Yours is the voice of a new world;
And all the hills burn with such blinding art

That Christ and angels walk among us, everywhere.
These are their ways, their fiery footsteps,
That flash and vanish, smile and pass;
—By those bright passengers our groves are all inspired.
Lo, we have seen you, we have seized you, wonder,
Caught you, half held you in the larch and lighted birch:
But in that capture you have sailed us half-mile-high into
    the air

To taste the silences of the inimitable hawk:
But in the dazzled, high and unelectric air
Seized in the talons of the terrible Dove,
The huge, unwounding Spirit,
We suddenly escape the drag of earth
Fly from the dizzy paw of gravity
And swimming in the wind that lies beyond the track
Of thought and genius and of desire,

Trample the white, appalling stratosphere.

Αντιρηοπ

Lord, what is the secret of this world that does not own
itself and is not owned by you, as by a user, by a proprietor?

The Lord God is present where the new day shines
in the moisture on the young grasses.
The Lord God is present where the small wildflowers
are known to Him alone.
The Lord God passes suddenly, in the wind,
at the moment when night ebbs into the ground.
He Who is infinitely great has given to His children
a share in His own innocence.
His alone is the gentlest of loves: whose pure flame
respects all things.
God, Who owns all things, leaves them all to themselves.
He never takes them for His own,
the way we take them for our own and destroy them.
He leaves them to themselves.
He keeps giving to them, giving them all that they are,
asking no thanks of them save that they should receive
from Him
and be loved and nurtured by Him,
and that they should increase and multiply,
and so praise Him.
He saw that all things were good, and He did not enjoy
them.
He saw that all things were beautiful and He did not want
them.
His love is not like ours. His love is unpossessive.
His love is pure because it needs nothing.

Psalm Prayer

The most wonderful thing about the world is that it is nobody's property, not even God's! We who are ruined by our own indigence to the point of thinking that we can possess something worship a false god, a god of possession, that is, a god of destruction. God is the God of the living.

Reading

Sunrise is an event that calls forth solemn music in the very depths of man's nature, as if one's whole being had to attune itself to the cosmos and praise God for the new day, praise Him in the name of all the creatures that ever were or ever will be.

I look at the rising sun and feel that now upon me falls the responsibility of seeing what all my ancestors have seen, in the Stone Age and even before it, praising God before me. Whether or not they praised Him then, for themselves, they must praise Him now in me. When the sun rises each one of us is summoned by the living and the dead to praise God.

Silence

RESPONSORY

Although we know no hills, no country rivers,
Here in the jungles of our waterpipes and iron ladders,
Our thoughts are quieter than rivers,
Our loves are simpler than the trees,
Our prayers deeper than the sea.

CANTICLE

We have found, we have found,
the places where the rain is deep and silent.
We have found the fountains of the spring,
where the Lord emerges refreshed every morning!
He has laid His hand upon our shoulders,
and our heart, like a bird, has spoken!

INTERCESSIONS

THE LORD'S PRAYER

CLOSING PRAYER

Father, Father, Whom we thought so hidden
Somewhere behind the jealous walls of Mars,
Oh how You visit us, at the deep roots of life,
With glad reprisals.

Day

Plenty of time! Plenty of time! No breaking your neck to get things done before the next thing happens.

Exhortation

The real job is to lay the groundwork for a deep change of heart on the part of the whole nation so that one day it can really go through the *metanoia* we need for a peaceful world.

Meditation

Believe in deep union and agreement with the forces of life and hope that are struggling for the renewal of the true cultural and spiritual vitality of the "new work." The forces of life must win. And Christians must rediscover the truth that the Cross is the sign of life, renewal, affirmation and joy, not of death, repression, negation and the refusal of life. We must not refuse the providential opportunities that come to us in the midst of darkness.

I am not a pure pacifist in theory, though today in practice I don't see how one can be anything else since limited wars (however "just") present an almost certain danger of nuclear war on an all-out scale. It is absolutely clear to me that we are faced with the obligation, both as human beings and as Christians, of striving in every way possible to abolish war. The magnitude of the task cannot be allowed to deter us. Even if it seems impossible, we must still attempt it. This demands of course a spirit of faith.

I believe the only really valid thing that can be accomplished in the direction of world peace and unity at the moment is the preparation of the way by the formation of men who, isolated, perhaps not accepted or understood by any "movement," are able to unite in themselves and experience in their own lives all that is best and most true in the various great spiritual traditions. Such men can become as it were "sacraments" or signs of peace, at least. They can do much to open up the minds of their contemporaries to receive, in the future, new seeds of thought. Our task is one of very remote preparation, a kind of arduous and unthanked pioneering.

PRAYER

Our hearts are heavens
Andour eyes are light-years deep,
Sounding Your will, Your peace, in its unbounded fathoms:

Oh balance all our turning orbits, till that morning,
Upon the center and level of Your holy love:
Then lock our souls forever in the nucleus of its Law.

LESSON

It seems to me that the basic problem is not political, it is
apolitical and human. One of the most important things to
do is to keep cutting deliberately through political lines and
barriers and emphasizing the fact that these are largely fabri-
cations and that there is another dimension, a genuine reality, totally opposed to the fictions of politics: the human
dimension which politics pretend to arrogate entirely to
themselves. This is the necessary first step along the long
way toward the perhaps impossible task of purifying,
humanizing and somehow illuminating politics themselves.
Is this possible? At least we must try to hope in that, otherwise all is over. But politics as they now stand are hopeless.

Hence the desirability of a manifestly non-political witness,
non-aligned, non-labeled, fighting for the reality of man and
his rights and needs in the nuclear world in some measure
against all the alignments.

COLLECT

The fool is one
Who strives to procure at each instant
Some result
That Allah has not willed.

Examen

One of our great problems is to see clearly what we have to resist. I would say that at the moment we have to understand better than we do the war mentality. If we do not understand it, we will run the risk of contributing to its confusions and thereby helping the enemies of man and of peace. The great danger is that under the pressures of anxiety and fear, the alternation of crisis and relaxation and new crisis, the people of the world will come to accept gradually the idea of war, the idea of submission to total power, and the abdication of reason, spirit and individual conscience. The great peril is the deadening of conscience.

Kyrie

Keep me, above all things, from sin.

Stanch me in the rank wound of covetousness
and the hungers that exhaust my nature with their bleeding.
Stamp out the serpent envy that stings love with poison
and kills all joy.
Untie my hand and deliver my heart from sloth.

Set me free from the laziness that goes about disguised
as activity
when activity is not required of me,
and from cowardice that does what it is not demanded,
in order to escape sacrifice.

And then to wait in peace and emptiness and oblivion
of all things.

Benediction

Let us hope that what we will see in the next few years will surprise us by being less bad than we fear, and that God may show His Face and His truth in our history, in spite of the pride of men. And that we may reach a period of peaceful development, if it be possible.

DUSK

*Now I am grown-up and have not
time for anything but the essentials.*

OPENING VERSE

Teach me to take all grace
And spring it into blades of act,
Grow spears and sheaves of charity,
While each new instant, (new eternity)
Flowering with clean and individual
circumstance,
Speaks me the whisper of His consecrating Spirit.
Then will obedience bring forth new Incarnations
Shining to God with the features of His Christ.

EVENING HYMN

For the sound of my Beloved,
The voice of the sound of my Three Beloved
(One of my Three of my One Beloved)
Comes down out of the heavenly depths

And hits my heart like thunder:
And lo! I am alive and dead
With heart held fast in that Three-Personed Love.
And lo! God, my God!
Look! Look! I travel in Thy strength
I swing in the grasp of Thy Love, Thy great Love's
    One Strength,
I run Thy swift ways, Thy straightest rails
Until my life becomes Thy Life and sails or rides
    like an express!

Antiphon

How far have I to go to find you in whom I have already arrived!

Psalm

Today, in a moment of trial, I rediscovered Jesus,
or perhaps discovered Him for the first time.
I came closer than ever to fully realizing how true it is
that our relations with Jesus are something utterly beyond
the level of imagination and emotion.

His eyes, which are the eyes of Truth, are fixed
    upon my heart.
Where His glance falls, there is peace:
for the light of His Face, which is the Truth,
produces truth wherever it shines.

There too is joy:
And he says to those he loves,
I will fix my eyes upon you.

His eyes are always on us everywhere and in all times.
No grace comes to us from heaven except He looks
  upon our hearts.

The grace of this gaze of Christ upon my heart
transfigured this day like a miracle.
It seems to me that I have discovered a freedom that I never
  knew before in my life.

I have felt that the Spirit of God was upon me,
and I thought that,
if I only turned my head a little,
I would see a tremendous host of angels in silver armor
advancing behind me through the sky,
coming at last to sweep the whole world clean.
It carried me along on a vivid ocean of peace.

And the whole world and the whole sky was filled
  with wonderful music,
As it has often been for me in these days.

Psalm Prayer

My Lord, You have heard the cry of my heart because it was
You Who cried out within my heart.

Epistle

The language of Christianity has been so used and so mis-
used that sometimes you distrust it: you do not know
whether or not behind the word "Cross" there stands the
experience of mercy and salvation, or only the threat of
punishment. If my word means anything to you, I can say to

you that I have experienced the Cross to mean mercy and not cruelty, truth and not deception: that the news of the truth and love of Jesus is indeed the true good news, but in our time it speaks out in strange places. And perhaps it speaks out in you more than it does in me: perhaps Christ is nearer to you than He is to me: this I say without shame or guilt because I have learned to rejoice that Jesus is in the world in people who know Him not, that He is at work in them when they think themselves far from Him, and it is my joy to tell you to hope though you think that for you of all hope is impossible. Hope not because you think you can be good, but because God loves us irrespective of our merits and whatever is good in us comes from His love, not from our own doing. Hope because Jesus is with those who are poor and outcasts and perhaps despised even by those who should seek them and care for them most lovingly because they act in God's name. No one on earth has reason to despair of Jesus because Jesus loves man, loves him in his sin, and we too must love man in his sin.

Silence

Responsory

It is Our Lady who is working in me in these days,
trying to awaken in me, bring out new worlds to light,
    draw me into her Christ
Who is the center of all. And she does this when I go to
    her.

Ashes of paper, ashes of a world
Wandering, when fire is done:
We argue with the drops of rain!

Until One comes Who walks unseen
Even in elements we have destroyed.
Deeper than any nerve
He enters flesh and bone.
Planting His truth, He puts our substance on.
Air, earth and rain
Rework the frame that fire has ruined.
What was dead is waiting for His Flame.
Sparks of His Spirit spend their seeds, and hide
To grow like irises, born before summertime.
These blue things bud in Israel.

The girl prays by the bare wall
Between the lamp and the chair.
(Framed with an angel in our galleries
She has a richer painted room, sometimes a crown.
Yet seven pillars of obscurity
Build her to Wisdom's house, and Ark, and Tower.
She is the Secret of another Testament
She owns their manna in her jar.)

Fifteen years old—
The flowers printed on her dress
Cease moving in the middle of her prayer
When God, Who sends the messenger,
Meets His messenger in her Heart.

Her answer, between breath and breath,
Wrings from her innocence our Sacrament!
In her white body God becomes our Bread.

Intercessions

Almighty and merciful God, Father of all, Creator and Ruler of the Universe, Lord of History, whose designs are inscrutable, whose glory is without blemish, whose compassion is inexhaustible, in your will is our peace.

> Teach us to be long-suffering in anguish and insecurity.
> Teach us to wait and trust.
> Grant light, grant strength and patience to all who work for peace,
> To this Congress, our President, our military forces, and our adversaries.
> Grant us to see your face in the lightning of this cosmic storm,

O God of holiness,
Grant us to seek peace where it is truly found!
In your will, O God, is our peace!

Closing Prayer

My Lord God, I have no idea where I am going. I do not see
the road ahead of me.
I cannot know for certain where it will end.
Nor do I really know myself, and the fact that I think I am
following your will does not mean that I am actually
doing so.
But I believe that the desire to please you does in fact
please you.
And I hope that I have that desire in all that I am doing.
I hope that I will never do anything apart from that desire.
And I know that if I do this you will lead me by the right
road, though I may know nothing about it.
Therefore I will trust you always though I may seem to be
lost and in the shadow of death.
I will not fear for you are ever with me, and you will never
leave me to face my perils alone.

DARK

No clock:
Only the Heart's blood
Only the word.

OPENING VERSE

 think poetry must
I think it must
Stay open all night
In beautiful cellars.

NIGHT HYMN

Now, in the middle of the limpid evening,
The moon speaks clearly to the hill.
The wheatfields make their simple music,
Praise the quiet sky.

And down the road, the way the stars come home,
The cries of children

Play on the empty air, a mile or more,
And fall on our deserted hearing,
Clear as water.

They say the sky is made of glass,
They say the smiling moon's a bride.
They say they love the orchards and apple trees,
The trees, their innocent sisters, dressed in blossoms,
Still wearing, in the blurring dusk,
White dresses from that morning's first communion.

And, where blue heaven's fading fire last shines
They name the new come planets
With words that flower
On little voices, light as stems of lilies.

And where blue heaven's fading fire last shines,
Reflected in the poplar's ripple,
One little, wakeful bird
Sings like a shower.

Antiphon

Up with the revolution of tulips. Tulips are not important,
they are essential. Yes, sing. Love and Peace, silence, movement of planets.

Psalm

Lord, when there is no escape, be my Defender
When they crowd around me, Lord
Be my Defender,

Steal me out of here,
Have mercy Lord, show your power
Steal me out of here,
Be my Defender.

Man
Crowding all around
Why are you
So cold, so proud

Why is your tongue so mean
Why is your hand
So quick to harm
Why are you like
A rattlesnake
So quick to strike?

Man
Crowding all around
You have children in your home
You have looked for happiness
You have asked the Lord
For better days
Kneel and tremble in the night
Ask my Lord to change your heart
Fear my Lord and learn the ways
Of patience, love and sacrifice.

Lord, when they all go by, riding high
Looking down on me, be my Defender
Be my Defender, Lord
And my secret heart will know

A sweeter joy, Lord, a sweeter joy
For I'll walk alone
With only you
I'll lie down to sleep in peace, in hope
For though I cannot trust in Man
I trust in you.

> Lord, when they all go by
> Riding high
> Looking down on me
> Be my Defender,
> Lord, be my Defender.

PSALM PRAYER

There should be at least a room, or some corner where no one will find you and disturb you or notice you. You should be able to untether yourself from the world and set yourself free, loosing all the fine strings and strands of tension that bind you, by sight, by sound, by thought, to the presence of other men. "But thou, when thou shalt pray, enter into thy chamber, and having shut the door, pray to thy Father in secret. . . ." Once you have found such a place, be content with it, and do not be disturbed if a good reason takes you out of it. Love it, and return to it as soon as you can, and do not be quick to change it for another.

SILENCE

Litany

Learn how to meditate on paper. Drawing and writing are forms of meditation.
Learn how to contemplate works of art.
Learn how to pray in the streets or in the country.
Know how to meditate not only when you have a book in your hand
But when you are waiting for a bus or riding in the train.
Above all, enter into the liturgy and make the liturgical cycle a part of your life—
Let its rhythm work its way into your body and soul.

Closing Prayer

Let there be a place somewhere in which you can breathe naturally, quietly, and not have to take your breath in continuous short gasps. A place where your mind can be idle, and forget its concerns, descend into silence, and worship the Father in secret.

There can be no contemplation where there is no secret.

†HURSDAY

Dawn

I am the appointed hour,
The "now" that cuts
Time like a blade

Opening Verse

ne lovely dawn after another. Such peace!
Meditation with fireflies, mist in the valley, last
quarter of the moon, distant owls—gradual
inner awakening and centering in peace and
harmony of love and gratitude.

Hymn

When the full fields begin to smell of sunrise
And the valleys sing in their sleep,
The pilgrim moon pours over the solemn darkness
Her waterfalls of silence,
And then departs,
up the long avenue of trees.

The stars hide, in the glade, their light, like tears,
And tremble where some train runs, lost,
Baying in eastward mysteries of distance,
Where fire flares, somewhere, over a sink of cities.

Now kindle in the windows of this ladyhouse, my soul,
Your childish, clear awakeness:
Burn in the country night
Your wise and sleepless lamp.
For, from the frowning tower, the windy belfry,
Sudden the bells come, bridegrooms,
And fill the echoing dark with love and fear.

Sink from your shallows, soul, into eternity,
And slake your wonder at that deep-lake spring.
We touch the rays we cannot see,
We feel the light that seems to sing.

Antiphon

The fire of a wild white sun has eaten up the distance
between hope and despair.

Dance in this sun, you tepid idiot. Wake up and dance in the
clarity of perfect contradiction.

Psalm

By ceasing to question the sun I have become light,
Bird and wind.

My leaves sing.

I am earth, earth

All these lighted things
Grow from my heart.

A tall, spare pine
Stands like the initial of my first
Name when I had one.

When I had a spirit,
When I was on fire
When this valley was
Made out of fresh air
You spoke my name
In naming Your silence:
O sweet, irrational worship!
I am earth, earth

My heart's love
Bursts with hay and flowers.
I am a lake of blue air
In which my own appointed place
Field and valley
Stand reflected.

I am earth, earth

Out of my grass heart Rises the bobwhite.
Out of my nameless weeds His foolish worship.

PSALM PRAYER

You fool, it is life that makes you dance: have you forgotten?
Come out of the smoke, the world is tossing in its sleep, the
sun is up, the land is bursting in the silence of dawn. The

gentle earth relaxes and spreads out to embrace the strong sun. The grasses and flowers speak their own secret names.

Reading

To say that I am made in the image of God is to say that love is the reason for my existence, for God is love. Love is my true identity. Selflessness is my true self. Love is my true character. Love is my name.

If, therefore, I do anything or think anything or say anything or know anything that is not purely for the love of God, it cannot give me peace, or rest, or fulfillment, or joy.

To find love I must enter into the sanctuary where it is hidden, which is the mystery of God.

Silence

Responsory

O great God, Father of all things, Whose infinite light is darkness to me, Whose immensity is to me as the void, You have called me forth out of yourself because You love me in Yourself, and I am a transient expression of Your inexhaustible and eternal reality. I could not know You, I would be lost in this darkness, I would fall away from You into this void, if You did not hold me to Yourself in the Heart of Your only begotten Son.

Canticle

If you seek a heavenly light
I, Solitude, am your professor!
I go before you into emptiness,
Raise strange suns for your new mornings,
Opening the windows
Of your innermost apartment.
When I, loneliness, give my special signal
Follow my silence, follow where I beckon!
Fear not, little beast, little spirit
(Thou word and animal)
I, Solitude, am angel
And have prayed in your name.

Look at the empty, wealthy night
The pilgrim moon!
I am the appointed hour,
The "now" that cuts
Time like a blade.
I am the unexpected flash
Beyond "yes," beyond "no,"
The forerunner of the Word of God.

Follow my ways and I will lead you
To golden-haired suns,
Logos and music, blameless joys,
Innocent of questions
And beyond answers:

For I, Solitude, am thine own self:
I, Nothingness, am thy All.
I, Silence, am thy Amen!

Intercessions

The Lord's Prayer

Closing Prayer

O God, give peace to Your world. Give strength to the hearts of men. Raise us up from death in Christ. Give us to eat His immortality and His glory. Give us to drink the wine of His Kingdom.

DAY

Take more time, cover less ground.

EXHORTATION

ot to be without words in a season of effort.
Not to be without a vow in the summer of
harvest.
What have the signs promised on the lonely
hill?

Word and work have their measure, and so does pain.
Look in your own life and see if you find it.

MEDITATION

All day I have been waiting for You with my faculties bleeding the poison of unsuppressed activity. I have waited for

Your silence and Your peace to stanch and cleanse them, O my Lord.

You will heal my soul when it pleases You, because I have trusted in You.

I will no longer wound myself with the thoughts and questions that have surrounded me like thorns: that is a penance You do not ask of me.

You have made my soul for Your peace and Your silence, but it is lacerated by the noise of my activity and my desires. My mind is crucified all day by its own hunger for experience, for ideas, for satisfaction. And I do not possess my house in silence.

But I was created for Your peace and You will not despise my longing for the holiness of Your deep silence. O my Lord, You will not leave me forever in this sorrow, because I have trusted in You and I will wait upon Your good pleasure in peace and without complaining any more. This, for Your glory.

Prayer

Good Shepherd, You have a wild and crazy sheep in love with thorns and brambles. But please don't get tired of looking for me! I know You won't. For You have found me. All I have to do is stay found.

Lesson

There is a silent self within us whose presence is disturbing precisely because it is so silent: it *can't* be spoken. It has to

147

remain silent. To articulate it, to verbalize it, is to tamper with it, and in some ways to destroy it.

Now let us frankly face the fact that our culture is one which is geared in many ways to help us evade any need to face this inner, silent self. We live in a state of constant semiattention to the sound of voices, music, traffic, or the generalized noise of what goes on around us all the time. This keeps us immersed in a flood of racket and words, a diffuse medium in which our consciousness is half diluted: we are not quite "thinking," not entirely responding, but we are more or less there. We are not fully present and not entirely absent; not fully withdrawn, yet not completely available. It cannot be said that we are really participating in anything and we may, in fact, be half conscious of our alienation and resentment. Yet we derive a certain comfort from the vague sense that we are "part of something"—although we are not quite able to define what that something is—and probably wouldn't want to define it even if we could. We just float along in the general noise. Resigned and indifferent, we share semiconsciously in the mindless mind of Muzak and radio commercials which passes for "reality."

Collect

My mind is scattered among things, not because of my work, but because I am not detached and I do not attend first of all to God. On the other hand, I do not attend to Him because I am so absorbed in all these objects and events. I have to wait on His grace. But how stubborn and slow my nature is. And how I keep confusing myself and complicating things for myself by useless twisting and turning.

What I need most of all is the grace to really accept God as He gives Himself to me in every situation.

Examen

I do have a past to break with, an accumulation of inertia, waste, wrong, foolishness, rot, junk, a great need of clarification of mindfulness, or rather of no mind—a return to genuine practice, right effort, need to push on to the great doubt. Need of the Spirit.

Hang on to the clear light!

Kyrie

This is what it means to seek God perfectly:
to withdraw
from illusion and pleasure,
from worldly anxieties and desires,
from the works that God does not want,
from a glory that is only human display;
to keep my mind free from confusion in order that
    my liberty may be always at the disposal of His will;
to entertain silence in my heart and listen for the
    voice of God.

And then to wait in peace and emptiness and oblivion
    of all things.

Sapiennia [wisdom]. To know and taste the secret good that is present but is not known to those who, because they are restless and because they are discontent and because they complain, cannot apprehend it. The present good—reality—God. *Gustate et videte.* [taste and see].

DUSK

....

Christ has laid hold upon time and sanctified it, giving it a sacramental character, a sign of our union with God.

OPEⴖIⴖG VERSE

ake ready for the Face that speaks like lightning,
Uttering the new name of your exultation
Deep in the vitals of your soul.
Make ready for the Christ, Whose smile,
  like lightning,
Sets free the song of everlasting glory
That now sleeps, in your paper flesh, like dynamite.

EVEⴖIⴖG HYMⴖ

Praises and canticles anticipate
Each day the singing bells that wake the sun,
But now our psalmody is done.

The Truth that transubstantiates the body's night
Has made our minds His temple-tent:
Open the secret eye of faith
And drink these deeps of invisible light.

The weak walls
Of the world fall
And heaven, in floods, comes pouring in:

Sink from your shallows, soul, into eternity,
And slake your wonder at that deep-lake spring.
We touch the rays we cannot see,
We feel the light that seems to sing.

Antiphon

Sow some light winds upon the acres of our spirit,
And cool the regions where our prayers are reapers,
And slake us, Heaven, with Your living rivers.

Psalm

In the center of our being is a point of nothingness
which is untouched by sin and by illusion,

a point of pure truth,
a point or spark which belongs entirely to God,
which is never at our disposal,
from which God disposes of our lives,
which is inaccessible to the fantasies of our own mind
or the brutalities of our own will.

This little point of nothingness and of absolute poverty
is the pure glory of God in us.

It is like a pure diamond, blazing with the invisible light of
    heaven.
It is in everybody, and if we could see it
we would see these billions of points of light
coming together in the face and blaze of a sun
that would make all the darkness and cruelty of life vanish
    completely.

I have no program for this seeing.
It is only given.

But the gate of heaven is everywhere.

PSALM PRAYER

Love comes out of God and gathers us to God in order to
pour itself back into God through all of us and bring us all
back to Him on the tide of His own infinite mercy.

So we all become doors and windows through which God
shines back into His own house.

EPISTLE

God is not a "problem" and we who live the contemplative
life have learned by experience that one cannot know God as
long as one seeks to solve "the problem of God." To seek to
solve the problem of God is to seek to see one's own eyes.
One cannot see his own eyes because they are that with
which he sees and God is the light by which we see—by
which we see not a clearly defined "object" called God, but
everything else in the invisible One. God is then the Seer
and the Seeing, but on earth He is not seen. In heaven, He is

the Seer, the Seeing and the Seen. God seeks Himself in us, and the aridity and sorrow of our heart is the sorrow of God who is not known in us, who cannot find Himself in us because we do not dare to believe or trust the incredible truth that He could live in us, and live there out of choice, out of preference. But indeed we exist solely for this, to be the place He has chosen for His presence, His manifestation in the world, His epiphany. But we make all this dark and inglorious because we fail to believe it, we refuse to believe it. It is not that we hate God, rather that we hate ourselves, despair of ourselves: if we once began to recognize, humbly but truly, the real value of our own self, we would see that this value was the sign of God in our being, the signature of God upon our being. Fortunately, the love of our fellow man is given us as the way of realizing this. For the love of our brother, our sister, our beloved, our wife, our child, is there to see with the clarity of God Himself that we are good. It is the love of my lover, my brothers or my child that sees God in me, makes God credible to myself in me. And it is my love for my lover, my child, my brother, that enables me to show God to him or her in himself or herself. Love is the epiphany of God in our poverty.

Silence

Responsory

As you have dealt with me, Lady, deal also with all my millions of brothers who live in the same misery that I knew then: lead them in spite of themselves and guide them by your tremendous influence, O Holy Queen of souls and refuge sinners, and bring them to your Christ the way you brought me. *Illos tuos misericordes oculos ad nos converte, et Jesum, bendictum fructum ventris tui, nobis ostende*, Show us your Christ, Lady, after this our exile, yes: but show him to us also now, show him to us here, while we are still wanderers.

MARIAN CANTICLE

But oh! Queen of all grace and counsel,
Cause of our joy, Oh Clement Virgin, come:
Show us those eyes as chaste as lightning,
Kinder than June and true as Scripture.
Heal with your looks the poisons of the universe,
And claim your Son's regenerate world!

Because your Christ disposed Orion and Andromeda
And ordered the clean spheres,
And interplayed the chiming suns to be your toy,
Charm you with antiphon and psalmody
And canticle, and countersong;

Because your Christ
Fired the fair stars with argent for your raiment,
And charged the sinner's tears
With clean repentent lights—
(As on the day you found me in the dens of libraries
And crushed the jeweled head of heresy)—
He gave you every one of the redeemed to be your dowry
And angels for your crown.

Come from the compass quarter where the thunder sleeps
And let the pity of those eyes
Rout all the armies of our million dangers

Here where we lie in siege:
For you unlock the treasures of the bleeding Wood.
You hold the Mass-keys, and the locks of Calvary,
And All-grace springs in the founts of your demand.

Intercessions

Almighty and merciful God, Father of all, Creator and Ruler of the Universe, Lord of History, whose designs are inscrutable, whose glory is without blemish, whose compassion for the errors of men is inexhaustible, in your will is our peace.

> Grant us prudence in proportion to our power,
> Wisdom in proportion to our science,
> Humaneness in proportion to our wealth and might.

Grant us to see your face in the lightning of this cosmic storm,
O God of holiness,
Grant us to seek peace where it is truly found!
In your will, O God, is our peace!

The Lord's Prayer

Closing Prayer

Oh God, in accepting one another wholeheartedly, fully, completely, we accept You, and we thank You, and we adore You, and we love You with our whole being, because our being is in Your being, our spirit is rooted in Your spirit. Fill us then with love, and let us be bound together with love as we go our diverse ways, united in this one spirit which makes You present in the world, and which makes You witness to the ultimate reality that is love. Love has overcome. Love is victorious. Amen.

DARK

The fullness of time is the time of our emptiness,
which draws Christ down into our lives,
so that in us and through us he may bring the
fullness of his truth to the world.

Opening Verse

h, listen to that darkness, listen to that deep
darkness,
Listen to those seas of darkness on whose
shores we stand and die.
Now can we have you, peace, now can we sleep
in Your will, sweet God of peace?
Now can we have Your Word and in Him rest?

Night Hymn

How long we wait, with minds as quiet as time,
Like sentries on a tower.
How long we watch, by night, like the astronomers.

Heaven, when will we hear you sing,
Arising from our grassy hills,
And say: "The dark is done, and Day
Laughs like a Bridegroom in His tent, the lovely sun,
His tent the sun, His tent the smiling sky!"

How long we wait with minds as dim as ponds
While stars swim slowly homeward in the water of our
    west!
Heaven, when will we hear you sing?

In the blue west the moon is uttered like the word:
    "Farewell."

Antiphon

You have to be all the time cooperating with love and love
sets a fast pace even at the beginning and, if you don't keep
up, you'll get dropped.

Psalm

O the Lord is good
To the steady man
He is good
To the man of peace.

But I stumbled, I stumbled in my mind
Over those men
I did not understand
Rich and fat
With big cigars and cars
They seem to have no trouble,
Know no pain
I do not understand those men of war
Strong and proud
Rich and fat
The more they have
The more they hate
And hate rolls down their skin
Like drops of sweat.

I stumbled, I stumbled in my mind
Over those men of war

Full of power
Rich and fat
The more they have, the more they hate
And they jeered
At my people
Showed their power
Rolled their pile of fat
And my people
Listened to their threat
My people was afraid
Of those men of war
When hate rolled down their skin
Like drops of sweat.

My heart was sore
Seeing their success
"Does God care?
Has He forgotten us?"
Lord, I nearly fell
Stumbling in my mind
About those men of war
It was hard to see
Till you showed me
How like a dream
Those phantoms pass away.

Psalm Prayer

There is not a flower that opens, not a seed that falls into the ground, and not an ear of wheat that nods on the end of its stalk in the wind that does not preach and proclaim the greatness and mercy of God to the whole world.

There is not an act of kindness or generosity, not an act of sacrifice done, or a word of peace and gentleness spoken, not a child's prayer uttered, that does not sing hymns to God.

Silence

Litany

All holy souls
pray for us
all Carmelites pray

all Third Orders
all sodalities,
all altar societies,
all action groups,
all inaction groups,
all beat up shut in groups,
all without money groups,

pray for the rich groups
vice versa
mutual help,
amen, amen.

Closing Prayer

And the deepest level of communication is not communication, but communion. It is wordless. It is beyond words, and it is beyond speech, and it is beyond concept. Not that we discover a new unity. We discover an older unity. My dear, we are already one. But we imagine that we are not. And what we have to recover is our original unity. What we have to be is what we are.

FRIDAY

Dawn

*Every golden instant mints the Christ
who keeps us free.*

Opening Verse

ut look: the valleys shine with promises,
And every burning morning is a prophecy of Christ
Coming to raise and vindicate
Even our sorry flesh.

Hymn

His are the mysteries which I expound
And mine the children whom His stars befriend.
Our Christ has cleanly built His sacred town.

What do the windows of His city say?
His innocence is written on your sky!

Come to the ark and stone
Come to the Holies where His work is done,
Dear hasty doves, transparent in His stuff!

Gather us God in honeycombs,
For brightness falls upon our dark.

Death owns a wasted kingdom.
Bless and restore the blind, straighten the broken limb.
These mended stones shall build Jerusalem.

Brown universe whose liturgy Sweetly consumes my bones.

Antiphon

Christ, from my cradle, I had known You everywhere, And
even though I sinned, I walked in You, and knew You were
my world: You were my life and air, and yet I would not own
You.

Psalm

Slowly slowly
Comes Christ through the garden
Speaking to the sacred trees
Their branches bear his light
Without harm

Slowly slowly
Comes Christ through the ruins
Seeking the lost disciple
A timid one
Too literate
To believe words
So he hides

Slowly slowly
Christ rises on the cornfields

It is only the harvest moon
The disciple
Turns over in his sleep
And murmurs:
"My regret!"

The disciple will awaken
When he knows history
But slowly slowly
The Lord of History
Weeps into the fire.

Psalm Prayer

I am Christ's lost cell
His childhood and desert age
His descent into hell.
Love without need and without name
Bleeds in the empty problem
And the spark without identity
Circles the empty ceiling.

Reading

One thing above all is important: the "return to the Father."

The Son came into the world and died for us, rose and ascended to the Father; sent us His Spirit, that in Him and with Him we might return to the Father.

That we might pass clean out of the midst of all that is transitory and inconclusive: return to the Immense, the Primordial, the Source, the unknown, to Him Who loves and knows, to the Silent, to the Merciful, to the Holy, to Him Who is All.

To seek anything, to be concerned with anything but this is only madness and sickness, for this is the whole meaning and heart of all existence, and in this all the affairs of life, all the needs of the world and of men, take on their right significance: all point to this one great return to the Source.

All goals that are not ultimate, all "ends of the line" that we can see and plan as "ends," are simply absurd, because they do not even begin. The "return" is the end beyond all ends, and the beginning of beginnings.

To "return to the Father" is not to "go back" in time, to roll up the scroll of history, or to reverse anything. It is a going forward, a going beyond, for merely to retrace one's steps would be a vanity on top of vanity, a renewal of the same absurdity in reverse.

Our destiny is to go on beyond everything, to leave everything, to press forward to the End and find in the End our Beginning, the ever-new Beginning that has no end.

To obey Him on the way, in order to reach Him in whom I have begun, who is the key and the end—because He is the Beginning.

SILENCE

RESPONSORY

Deep is the ocean, boundless sweetness, kindness, humility, silence of wisdom that is not abstract, disconnected, fleshless.

Awakening us gently when we have exhausted ourselves to night and to sleep. O Dawn of wisdom!

Canticle

The song of my Beloved beside the stream.
The birds descanting in their clerestories.
His skies have sanctified my eyes, His woods are clearer
 than the King's palace.
But the air and I will never tell our secret.

Christ has sanctified the desert and the wilderness shines
 with promise.
The land is first in simplicity and strength.
I had never before spoken freely or so intimately with
 woods, hills, buds, water and sky.
On this great day, however, they understood their position
 and they remained mute in the presence of the Beloved.
Only His light was obvious and eloquent.
My, brother and sister, the fight and the water.
The stump and the stone. The tables of rock.
The blue, naked sky.

Intercessions

The Lord's Prayer

Closing Prayer

Thank God for the hill, the sky, the morning sun, the manna on the ground which every morning renews our lives.

Day

···

*For the unredeemed, the wheel of time
itself is only a spiritual prison.*

Exhortation

 his day throw open all your houses, and forever.
And love, not fear, the many poor.

Meditation

Why should I want to be rich, when You were poor? Why
should I desire to be famous and powerful? Why should I
cherish in my heart a hope that devours me—the hope for
perfect happiness in this life—when such hope, doomed to
frustration, is nothing but despair?

My hope is in what the eye has never seen. Therefore, let me not trust in visible rewards.

My hope is in what the heart cannot feel. Therefore let me not trust in the feelings of my heart.

My hope is in what the hand has never touched. Do not let me trust what I can grasp between my fingers.

Death will loosen my grasp and my vain hope will be gone.

PRAYER

Let my trust be in Your mercy, not in myself. Let my hope be in Your love, not in health, or strength, or ability or human resources.

If I trust You, everything else will become, for me, strength, health, and support. Everything will bring me to heaven. If I do not trust You, everything will be my destruction.

LESSON

It is true that the materialistic society, the so-called culture that has evolved under the tender mercies of capitalism, has produced what seems to be the ultimate limit of this worldliness. And nowhere, except perhaps in the analogous society of pagan Rome, has there ever been such a flowering of cheap and petty and disgusting lusts and vanities as in the world of capitalism, where there is no evil that is not fostered and encouraged for the sake of making money. We live in a society whose whole policy is to excite every nerve in the human body and keep it at the highest pitch of artificial tension, to strain every human desire to the limit and to create as many new desires and synthetic passions as possible, in order to cater to them with the products of our factories and printing presses and movie studios and all the rest.

No matter what happens, I feel myself more and more closely united with those who, everywhere, devote themselves to the glory of God's truth, to the search for divine values hidden among the poor and the outcast, to the love of that cultural heritage without which man cannot be healthy. The air of the world is foul with lies, hypocrisy, falsity, and life is short, death approaches. We must devote ourselves with generosity and integrity to the real values: there is no time for falsity and compromise. But on the other hand we do not have to be greatly successful or even well known. It is enough for our integrity to be known to God. What we do that is pure in His sight will avail for the liberty, the enlightenment, and the salvation of His children everywhere.

Collect

Let go of all that seems to suggest getting somewhere, being someone, having a name and a voice, following a policy and directing people in "my" ways. What matters is to *love*.

Examen

Wrestling quietly with the circumstances of my life. There is an attitude to be taken, there are decisions to be made. There is a radical refusal demanded of me somewhere and I do not know where it begins and ends and how to approach it.

God makes us ask ourselves questions most often when He intends to resolve them. He gives us needs that He alone can satisfy and awakens capacities that He means to fulfill. Any perplexity is liable to be a spiritual gestation, leading to a new birth and mystical generation.

Kyrie

This is what it means to seek God perfectly:

> to cultivate an intellectual freedom from the images of created things in order to receive the secret contact of God in obscure love;
> to love all as myself;
> to rest in humility and to find peace in withdrawal from conflict and competition;
> to turn aside from controversy and put away heavy loads of judgment and censorship and criticism and the whole burden of opinions that I have no obligation to carry.

And then to wait in peace and emptiness and oblivion of all things.

Benediction

I am the utter poverty of God. I am His emptiness, littleness, nothingness, lostness.
When this is understood, my life in His freedom, the self-emptying of God in me is the fullness of grace.
A love for God that knows no reason because He is the fullness of grace.
A love for God that knows no reason because He is God;
a love without measure, a love for God as personal.

Dusk

Some days in prayer Your Love
Delivers us from measure and from
time,
Melts all the barriers that stop our
passage to eternity
And solve the hours our chains.

Opening Verse

 hear a sovereign talking in my arteries
Reversing, with His Promises, all things
That now go on with fire and thunder.
His Truth is greater than disaster.
His Peace imposes silence on the evidence
against us.

Evening Hymn

Go tell the earth to shake
And tell the thunder
To wake the sky

And tear the clouds apart
Tell my people to come out
And wonder

Where the old world is gone
For a new world is born
And all my people
Shall be one.

So tell the earth to shake
With marching feet

Of messengers of peace
Proclaim my law of love
To every nation
Every race.

For the old wrongs are over
The old days are gone
A new world is rising
Where my people shall be one.

So tell the earth to shake
With marching feet
Of messengers of peace
Proclaim my law of love
To every nation
Every race.

And say
The old wrongs are over
The old ways are done
There shall be no more hate

And no more war
My people shall be one.

So tell the earth to shake
With marching feet
Of messengers of peace
Proclaim my law of love
To every nation
Every race.

For the old world is ended
The old sky is torn Apart.
A new day is born
They hate no more

They do not go to war
My people shall be one.

So tell the earth to shake
With marching feet
Of messengers of peace
Proclaim my law of love
To every nation
Every race.

There shall be no more hate
And no more oppression
The old wrongs are done
My people shall be one.

Antiphon

We are already one. But we imagine that we are not. And
what we have to recover is our original unity.

There is another kind of justice than the justice of number,
which can neither forgive nor be forgiven.
There is another kind of mercy than the mercy of Law
which knows no absolution.

There is a justice of newborn worlds which cannot
be counted.
There is a mercy of individual things that spring into
being without reason.
They are just without reason, and their mercy is without
explanation.

They have received rewards beyond description
because they themselves refuse to be described.
They are virtuous in the sight of God
because their names do not identify them.

Every plant that stands in the light of the sun is a saint
and an outlaw.
Every tree that brings forth blossoms without the
command of man
is powerful in the sight of God.
Every star that man has not counted
is a world of sanity and perfection.
Every blade of grass is an angel singing in a shower of glory.

These are worlds of themselves.
No man can use or destroy them.
Theirs is the life that moves without being seen and cannot
be understood.

It is useless to look for what is everywhere.
It is hopeless to hope for what cannot be,
gained because you already have it.

Psalm Prayer

This is the word You utter
To search our being to its roots:
This is the judgement and the question
And the joy we suffer:
This is our trial, this the weight of gladness that we cannot
   bear.

Epistle

The contemplative life is then the search for peace not in an abstract exclusion of all outside reality, not in a barren negative closing of the senses upon the world, but in the openness of love. It begins with the acceptance of my own self in my poverty and my nearness to despair in order to recognize that where God is there can be no despair, and God is in me even if I despair. That nothing can change God's love for me, since my very existence is the sign that God loves me and the presence of His love creates and sustains me. Nor is there any need to understand how this can be or to explain it or to solve the problems it seems to raise. For there is in our hearts and in the very ground of our being a natural certainty which is co-extensive with our very existence: a certainty that says that insofar as we exist, we are penetrated through and through with the sense and reality of God even though we may be utterly unable to believe or experience this in philosophic or even religious terms.

O my brother, the contemplative is the man not who has fiery visions of the cherubim carrying God on their imagined chariot, but simply he who has risked his mind in the desert beyond language and beyond ideas where God is encountered in the nakedness of pure trust, that is to say in the surrender of our poverty and incompleteness in order no longer to clench our minds in a cramp upon themselves, as if thinking made us exist. The message of hope the contemplative offers you, then, brother, is not that you need to find your way through the jungle of language and problems that today surround God: but that whether you understand or not, God loves you, is present in you, lives in you, dwells in you, calls you, saves you, and offers you an understanding and light which are like nothing you ever found in books or heard in sermons. The contemplative has nothing to tell you except to reassure you and say that if you dare to penetrate your own silence and risk the sharing of that solitude with the lonely other who seeks God through you, then you will truly recover the light and the capacity to understand what is beyond words and beyond explanations because it is too close to be explained: it is the intimate union in the depths of your own heart, of God's spirit and your own secret inmost self, so that you and He are in all truth One Spirit. I love you, in Christ.

SILENCE

Responsory

I need to know Mary is still close to us and need her to be very close to me here, always.

My heart breaks with need of vision and help for the world.

Marian Canticle

Lady, the night is falling and the dark
Steals all the blood from the scarred west.
The stars come out and freeze my heart
With drops of untouchable music, frail as ice
And bitter as the new year's cross.

Where in the world has any voice
Prayed to you, Lady, for the peace that's in your power?
In a day of blood and many beatings
I see the governments rise up, behind the steel horizon,
And take their weapons and begin to kill.
Where in the world has any city trusted you?
Out where the soldiers camp the guns begin to thump
And another winter time comes down
To seal our years in ice.
The last train cries out
And runs in terror from this farmers' valley
Where all the little birds are dead.

The roads are white, the fields are mute
There are no voices in the wood
And trees make gallows up against the sharp-eyed stars.
Oh where will Christ be killed again
In the land of these dead men?

Lady, the night has got us by the heart
And the whole world is tumbling down.
Words turn to ice in my dry throat
Praying for a land without prayer,
Walking to you on water all winter
In a year that wants more war.

INTERCESSIONS

Almighty and merciful God, Father of all, Creator and Ruler of the Universe, Lord of History, whose designs are inscrutable, whose glory is without blemish, whose compassion is inexhaustible, in your will is our peace.

> Bless our earnest will to help all races and peoples to
>   travel, in friendship with us,
> Along the road to justice, liberty and lasting peace:
> But grant us above all to see that our ways
>   are not necessarily your ways,
> That we cannot fully penetrate the mystery
>   of your designs
> And that the very storm of power now raging
>   on this earth
> Reveals your will and your inscrutable decision.

Grant us to see your face in the lightning of this cosmic-storm,
O God of holiness,
Grant us to seek peace where it is truly found!
In your will, O God, is our peace!

The Lord's Prayer

Closing Prayer

Let us continue searching in the secret of our hearts for the purity and integrity of the spirit—that "spiritus" that is the result of the union of the soul with God in a new and pure being, full of truth, humble instrument of God in the world.

DARK

. . . .

Come back for a moment! Pray! Be
quiet! Rest in your God!

OPENING VERSE

he four roads make off in silence
Towards the four parts of the starry universe.
Time falls like manna at the corners of the
earth.
We have become more humble than the rocks,
More wakeful than the patient hills.

NIGHT HYMN

Geography comes to an end,
Compass has lost all earthly north,
Horizons have no meaning
Nor roads an explanation:

I cannot even hope for any special borealis
To rouse my darkness with a brief "Hurray"!

O flaming Heart,
Unseen and unimagined in this wilderness,

You, You alone are real, and here I've found You.
Here will I love and praise You in a tongueless death,
Until my white devoted bones,
Long bleached and polished by the winds of this Sahara,
Relive at Your command,
Rise and unfold the flowers of their everlasting spring.

Antiphon

Heart, in the long, daily buryings of anguish and of prayer,
Or when I seem to die on the dry burning stone,
    among the thorns,
It is no longer I, but You Who work and grow:
It is your life, not mine, that makes these new green blades
In the transforming of my soul.

Psalm

Here is how I sum it up:
    Heaven does nothing: its non-doing is its serenity.
    Earth does nothing: its non-doing is its rest.
    From the union of these two non-doings
    All actions proceed,
    All things are made,
    How vast, how invisible
    This coming-to-be!
All things come from somewhere!
How vast, how invisible
No way to explain it!
All beings in their perfection
Are born of non-doing.

Hence it is said:
"Heaven and earth do nothing
Yet there is nothing they do not do."
Where is the man who can attain
To this non-doing?

PSALM PRAYER

It becomes very important to remember that the quality of one's night depends on the thoughts of the day. Still, the quality of one's nights depends on the sanity of the day. I bring there the sins of the day into the light and darkness of truth to be adored without disguise —then I want to fly back to the disguises.

SILENCE

LITANY

Contemplation is not trance or ecstasy
not emotional fire and sweetness that come with religious
    exaltation
not enthusiasm, not the sense of being "seized" by an
    elemental force
and swept into liberation by mystical frenzy.
Contemplation is no pain-killer.

In the end the contemplative suffers the anguish of realizing that *he no longer knows what God is*;
this is a great gain,

because "God is not a *what*,"
not a "thing."

There is "no such thing" as God
because God is neither a "what" or a "thing"
but a pure "*Who*,"
the "Thou" before whom our inmost "I" springs
    into awareness.

Closing Prayer

But oh! How far have I to go to find You in Whom I have already arrived! For now, oh my God, it is to You alone that I can talk, because nobody else will understand. I cannot bring any other on this earth into the cloud where I dwell in Your light, that is, Your darkness, where I am lost and abashed. I cannot explain to any other the anguish which is Your joy nor the loss which is the Possession of You, nor the distance from all things which is the arrival in You, nor the death which is the birth in You because I do not know anything about it myself and all I know is that I wish it were over—I wish it were begun.

You have contradicted everything. You have left me in no-man's land.

SATURDAY

Dawn

Hagia Sophia

Now you are free to go in and out of infinity.

Opening Verse

There is in all visible things an invisible fecundity, a dimmed light,

a meek namelessness, a hidden wholeness.

This mysterious Unity and Integrity is Wisdom, the Mother of all, *Natura naturans*.

Hymn

There is in all things an inexhaustible sweetness and purity,
a silence that is a fount of action and joy.
It rises up in wordless gentleness and flows out to me
from the unseen roots of all created being,
welcoming me tenderly,
saluting me with indescribable humility.

This is at once my own being, my own nature,
and the Gift of my Creator's Thought and Art within me,
speaking as Hagia Sophia,
speaking as my sister, Wisdom.

Aᴨᴛíᴘʜoᴨ

I am awakened, I am born again at the voice of this my
    Sister,
sent to me from the depths of the divine fecundity.

Psᴀʟᴍ

At five-thirty in the morning I am dreaming in a very quiet
    room
when a soft voice awakens me from my dream.
I am like all mankind awakening from all the dreams
that ever were dreamed in all the nights of the world.
It is like the One Christ awakening in all the separate selves
that ever were separate and isolated and alone in all the
    lands of the earth.
It is like all minds coming back together into awareness
from all distractions, cross-purposes and confusions,
into unity of love.

It is like the first morning of the world
(when Adam, at the sweet voice of Wisdom
awoke from nonentity and knew her),
and like the Last Morning of the world
when all the fragments of Adam will return from death
at the voice of Hagia Sophia,
and will know where they stand.

Such is the awakening of one man,
one morning,
Awakening out of languor and darkness,
out of helplessness, out of sleep,
newly confronting reality and finding it to be gentleness.

It is like being awakened by Eve.
It is like being awakened by the Blessed Virgin.
It is like coming forth from primordial nothingness
and standing in clarity, in Paradise.

PSALM VERSE

Wisdom cries out to all who will hear
and she cries out particularly to the little,
to the ignorant and the helpless.

READING

Who is more little, who is more poor than the helpless who
lies asleep in bed without awareness and without defense?
Who is more trusting than he who must entrust himself
each night to sleep? What is the reward of his trust?
Gentleness comes to him when he is most helpless and
awakens him, refreshed, beginning to be made whole. Love
takes him by the hand, and opens to him the doors of another life, another day.

(But he who has defended himself, fought for himself in
sickness, planned for himself, guarded himself, loved himself

alone and watched over his own life all night, is killed at last by exhaustion. For him there is no newness. Everything is stale and old.)

When the helpless one awakens strong at the voice of mercy, it is as if Life his Sister, as if the Blessed Virgin, (his own flesh, his own sister), as if Nature made wise by God's Art and Incarnation were to stand over him and invite him with unutterable sweetness to be awake and to live.

Silence

Responsory

This is what it means to recognize Hagia Sophia.

Canticle

O blessed, silent one, who speaks everywhere!

We do not hear the soft voice, the gentle voice, the merciful and feminine.
We do not hear mercy, or yielding love, or non-resistance, or non-reprisal.
In her there are no reasons and no answers.
Yet she is the candor of God's light, the expression of His simplicity.

We do not hear the uncomplaining pardon that bows down the innocent visages of flowers to the dewy earth.
We do not see the Child who is prisoner in all the people, and who says nothing.

She smiles, for though they have bound her,
she cannot be a prisoner.
Not that she is strong, or clever,
but simply that she does not understand imprisonment.

The helpless one, abandoned to sweet sleep, the gentle one
 will awake: Sophia.

All that is sweet in her tenderness will speak to him on all
 sides in everything, without ceasing,
and he will never be the same again.
He will have awakened not to conquest and dark pleasure
but to the impeccable pure simplicity of One
 consciousness
in all and through all:
one Wisdom, one Child, one Meaning, one Sister.

Intercessions

The Lord's Prayer

Closing Prayer

The stars rejoice in their setting, and in the rising of the Sun.
The heavenly lights rejoice in the going forth of one man to
make a new world in the morning, because he has come out
of the confused primordial dark night into consciousness.
He has expressed the clear silence of Sophia in his own
heart. He has become eternal.

Day

*Every day love corners me somewhere
and surrounds me with peace without
having to look very far or very hard or
do anything special.*

Exhortation

he Sun burns in the sky like the Face of God,
but we do not know his countenance as terrible. His light is diffused in the air and the light
of God is diffused by Hagia Sophia.

Meditation

We do not see the Blinding One in black emptiness.
He speaks to us gently in ten thousand things,
in which His light is one fullness and one Wisdom.

Thus He shines not on them but from within them.
Such is the loving-kindness of Wisdom.

All the perfections of created things are also in God;
and therefore He is at once Father and Mother.
As Father He stands in solitary might surrounded by
     darkness.
As Mother His shining is diffused, embracing all His
     creatures
with merciful tenderness and light.

Prayer

The Diffuse Shining of God is Hagia Sophia.
We call her His "glory."
In Sophia His power is experienced only as mercy
     and as love.

Lesson

Perhaps Sophia is the unknown, the dark, the nameless
Ousia. Perhaps she is even the Divine Nature, One in Father,
Son and Holy Ghost. And perhaps she is in infinite light
unmanifest, not even waiting to be known as Light. This I do
not know. Out of the silence Light is spoken. We do not
hear it or see it until it is spoken.

Collect

In the Nameless Beginning, without Beginning, was the
Light. We have not seen this Beginning. I do not know where
she is, in this Beginning. I do not speak of her as a
Beginning, but as a manifestation.

Examen

We do not hear the soft voice, the gentle voice, the merciful and feminine.

We do not see the Child who is prisoner in all the people.

Kyrie

This is what it means to seek God perfectly:
To have a will that is always ready to fold back within itself
and draw all the powers of the soul down from its deepest
    center
to rest in silent expectancy for the coming of God.

Poised in tranquil and effortless concentration upon the
    point of my dependence on Him,
to gather all that I am, and have all that I can possibly suffer
    or do or be,
and abandon them all to God in the resignation of a perfect
    love and blind faith and pure trust in God,
to do His will.

Benediction

Now the Wisdom of God, Sophia, comes forth, reaching from "end to end mightily." She wills to be also the unseen pivot of all nature, the center and significance of all the light that is *in* all and *for* all. That which is poorest and humblest, that which is most hidden in all things is nevertheless most obvious in them, and quite manifest, for it is their own self that stands before us, naked and without care.

DUSK

*The grip the present has on me. That
is the one thing that has grown most
noticeably in the spiritual life—
nothing much else.*

OPENING VERSE

Sophia, the feminine child, is playing in the
world,
obvious and unseen, playing at all times before
the Creator.

EVENING HYMN

Her delights are to be with the children of men. She is their
sister.
The core of life that exists in all things is tenderness, mercy,
virginity,
the Light, the Life considered as passive, as received,
as given, as taken,
as inexhaustibly renewed by the Gift of God.

Sophia is Gift, is Spirit, *Donum Dei.*
She is God-given and God Himself as Gift.
God as all, and God reduced to Nothing:
    inexhaustible nothingness.
Exinanivit semetipsum. Humility as the source of
    unfailing light.

Hagia Sophia in all things is the Divine Life reflected
    in them,
considered as a spontaneous participation,
as their invitation to the Wedding Feast.

Sophia is God's sharing of Himself with creatures.
His outpouring, and the Love by which He is given,
    and known, held and loved.

She is in all things like the air receiving the sunlight.
In her they prosper. In her they glorify God.
In her they rejoice to reflect Him. In her they are united
    with him.
She is the union between them. She is the Love that unites
    them.
She is life as communion, life as thanksgiving,
life as praise, life as festival, life as glory.

Because she receives perfectly there is in her no stain.
She is love without blemish, and gratitude without
    self-complacency.

Antiphon

All things praise her by being themselves and by sharing
    in the Wedding Feast.

She is the Bride and the Feast and the Wedding.

PSALM

The feminine principle in the world
is the inexhaustible source of creative realizations
    of the Father's glory.
She is His manifestation in radiant splendor!
But she remains unseen, glimpsed only by a few.
Sometimes there are none who know her at all.

Sophia is the mercy of God in us.
She is the tenderness with which the infinitely mysterious
    power of pardon
turns the darkness of our sins into the light of grace.
She is the inexhaustible fountain of kindness,
and would almost seem to be, in herself, all mercy.
So she does in us a greater work than that of Creation:
the work of new being in grace, the work of pardon,
the work of transformation from brightness to brightness
tamquam a Domini Spiritu.
She is in us the yielding and tender counterpart
of the power, justice and creative dynamism of the Father.

PSALM PRAYER

Now the Blessed Virgin Mary is the one created being who
enacts and shows forth in her life all that is hidden in
Sophia. Because of this she can be said to be a personal
manifestation of Sophia, Who in God is *Ousia* rather than
Person.

Epistle

Natura in Mary becomes pure Mother. In her, *Natura* is as she was from the origin, from her divine birth. In Mary *Natura* is all wise and is manifested as an all-prudent, all-loving, all-pure person: not a Creator, and not a Redeemer, but perfect Creature, perfectly Redeemed, the fruit of all God's great power, the perfect expression of wisdom in mercy.

Silence

Responsory

It is she, it is Mary, Sophia, who in sadness and joy, with the full awareness of what she is doing, sets upon the Second Person, the Logos, a crown which is His Human Nature. Thus her consent opens the door of created nature, of time, of history, to the Word of God.

Marian Canticle

God enters into His creation.
Through her wise answer, through her obedient
    understanding,
through the sweet yielding consent of Sophia,
God enters without publicity into the city
    of rapacious men.

She crowns Him not with what is glorious,
but with what is greater than glory:

the one thing greater than glory is weakness, nothingness,
    poverty.

She sends the infinitely Rich and Powerful One forth
as poor and helpless,
in His mission of inexpressible mercy,
to die for us on the Cross.

Intercessions

The Lord's Prayer

Closing Prayer

The shadows fall. The stars appear. The birds begin,
    to sleep.
Night embraces the silent half of the earth.
A vagrant, a destitute wanderer with dusty feet, finds his
    way down a new road.
A homeless God, lost in the night, without papers,
    without identification,
without even a number, a frail expendable exile
lies down in desolation under the sweet stars of the world
and entrusts Himself to sleep.

DARK

··

FIRE WATCH

Now is the time to meet you God.

OPENING VERSE

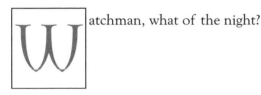

atchman, what of the night?

NIGHT HYMN

The night, O My Lord, is a time of freedom.

You have seen the morning and the night, and the night
    was better.
In the night all things began,
and in the night the end of all things has come before me.

I sit in darkness. I sit in human silence.
I begin to hear the eloquent night.

The world of this night resounds from heaven to hell with
    animal eloquence,
with the savage innocence of a million unknown creatures.

The enormous vitality of their music pounds and rings
    and throbs and echoes
until it gets into everything, and swamps the whole world in
    its neutral madness
which never becomes an orgy because all things are
    innocent, all things are pure.

The animals are the children of God and the night
    was made
to open infinite distances to charity and send our souls
    to play beyond the stars.

Antiphon

God, my God, God Whom I meet in darkness,
with You it is always the same thing!
Always the same question that nobody knows how to
answer!

Psalm

I have prayed to You in the daytime with thoughts
    and reasons,
and in the nighttime You have confronted me,
scattering thought and reason.

I have come to You in the morning with light
    and with desire,
and You have descended upon me, with great gentleness,
with most forbearing silence, in this inexplicable night,
dispersing light, defeating all desire.

I have explained to You a hundred times my motives
You have listened and said nothing,
and I have turned away and wept with shame.

Is it true that all my motives have meant nothing?
Is it true that all my desires were an illusion?

While I am asking questions which You do not answer,
You ask me a question which is so simple that I cannot
    answer.

I do not even understand the question.
This night, and every night, it is the same question.

· This nearness to You in the darkness is too simple
    and too close for excitement.
Your Reality, O God, speaks to my life as to an intimate,
    in the midst of a crowd of fictions:
Lord, God, the whole world tonight seems to be made
    out of paper.
The most substantial things are ready to crumble
    or tear apart and blow away.

Αптίρнοп

O God, my God, the night has values that day has never
dreamed of.

Psalm

All things stir by night,
waking or sleeping,
conscious of the nearness of their ruin.

Only man makes himself illuminations he conceives to be
solid and eternal.

But while we ask our questions and come to our decisions,
God blows our decisions out, the roofs of our houses cave
in upon us,
the tall towers are undermined by ants, the walls crack and
cave in,
and the holiest buildings burn to ashes
while the watchman is composing a theory of duration.

Now is the time to meet You, God, where the night is
wonderful,
where the forest opens out under the moon
and the living things sing terribly that only the present is
eternal
and that all things having a past and a future are doomed to
pass away!

I ask these useless questions,
I do not wait for an answer, because I have begun to realize
You never answer when I expect.

And now my whole being breathes the wind
and my hand is on the door through which I see the
heavens.

The door swings out upon a vast sea of darkness and of
    prayer.
Will it come like this, the moment of my death?
Will You open a door upon the great forest
and set my feet upon a ladder under the moon,
and take me out among the stars?

PSALM PRAYER

Lord God of this great night: do You see the woods?
Do You hear the rumor of their loneliness?
Do You behold their secrecy?
Do You remember their solitudes?
Do You see that my soul is beginning to dissolve like wax
    within me?

MEDITATION

But there is greater comfort in the substance of silence
than in the answer to a question.
Eternity is in the present.
Eternity is in the palm of the hand.
Eternity is a seed of fire,
whose sudden roots break barriers
that keep my heart from being an abyss.

The things of Time are in connivance with eternity.
The shadows serve You.
The beasts sing to You before they pass away.
The solid hills shall vanish like a worn-out garment.
All things change, and die and disappear.

Questions arrive, assume their actuality, and also disappear.
In this hour I shall cease to ask them,
and silence shall be my answer.
The world that Your love created,
and that my mind is always misinterpreting,
shall cease to interfere with our voices.

With You there is no dialogue
unless You choose a mountain and circle it with cloud
and print Your words in fire upon the mind of Moses.
What was delivered to Moses on tablets of stone,
as the fruit of lightning and thunder,
is now more thoroughly born in our own souls
as quietly as the breath of our own being.

The hand lies open. The heart is dumb.
The soul that held my substance together,
like a hard gem in the hollow of my own power,
will one day totally give in.

Although I see the stars, I no longer pretend to know them.
One by one I shall forget the names of individual things.

Litany

You, Who sleep in my breast, are not met with words,
but in the emergence of life within life
and of wisdom within wisdom.

You are found in communion:
Thou in me
and I in Thee
and Thou in them

and they in me:
dispossession within dispossession,
dispassion within dispassion,
emptiness within emptiness,
freedom within freedom.

I am alone.
Thou art alone.
The Father and I are One.

Closing Prayer

The Voice of God is heard in Paradise:

"What was vile has become precious. What is now precious
was never vile.
I have always known the vile as precious: for what is vile I
know not at all.

"What was cruel has become merciful. What is now merciful was never cruel.
I have always overshadowed Jonas with My mercy, and cruelty I know not at all.
Have you had sight of Me, Jonas My child?
Mercy within mercy within mercy.
I have forgiven the universe without end, because I have
never known sin.

"What was poor has become infinite. What is infinite was
never poor.
I have always known poverty as infinite: riches I love not at
all.

Prisons within prisons within prisons.
Do not lay up for yourselves ecstasies upon earth, where time and space corrupt,
where the minutes break in and steal.
No more lay hold on time, Jonas, My son, lest the rivers bear you away.

"What was fragile has become powerful. I loved what was most frail.
I looked upon what was nothing. I touched what was without substance,
and within what was not, I am."

POSTSCRIPT

Final Benediction

 hope these few words from me will be of some
help. I send you all my blessings and I join you
in your happiness. I am glad to have had some
small part in God's work for you.

ＮⵔＴＥＳ

Ａｂｂｒｅｖｉａｔｉｏｎｓ

AJ	The Asian Journal of Thomas Merton
BW	Bread in the Wilderness
CP	The Collected Poems of Thomas Merton
CGB	Conjectures of a Guilty Bystander
CWA	Contemplation in a World of Action
CT	The Courage for Truth
DBD	In The Dark Before Dawn
DWL	Dancing in the Water of Life
ES	Entering the Silence
HGL	The Hidden Ground of Love
LH	Life and Holiness
LL	Love and Living
LtL	Learning to Love
NM	The New Man
NMI	No Man Is an Island
NSC	New Seeds of Contemplation
OSM	The Other Side of the Mountain
PP	Passion for Peace
RJ	The Road to Joy
RM	Run to the Mountain
RU	Raids on the Unspeakable
SC	Seasons of Celebration
SCh	The School of Charity
SJ	The Sign of Jonas
SS	A Search for Solitude
SSM	The Seven Storey Mountain
TMR	A Thomas Merton Reader
TS	Thoughts in Solitude
TTW	Turning Toward the World
WS	The Waters of Siloe
WSD	Woods, Shore, Desert

ＦⵔＲⵔⵗⵔＲＤ

1.   HGL, 115

ＩⵏＴＲⵔＤⵓⵛＴⵉⵔⵏ

1.   NMI, 260
2.   HGL, 156
3.   "Psalm," CP, 220
4.   Ibid.
5.   ES, 456

6.   1 Thessalonians 5:17
7.   *SS*, 119
8.   *DWL*, 273
9.   *BW*, 55; 107
10.   *SS*, 119
11.   Ibid.
12.   "The Captives—A Psalm," *CP*, 212
13.   *RJ*, 89
14.   *NSC*, 25
15.   *NSC*, 38
16.   *ES*, 49
17.   *LL*, 24
18.   *ES*, 456
19.   *HGL*, 63–64, italics mine
20.   *DWL*, 347
21.   *NM*, 71ff.
22.   *"Hagia Sophia,"* *CP*, 363
23.   I borrow the metaphor from *Mythos Gate: A Book of Poems* by Ann Deignan
24.   *ES*, 473
25.   *CGB*, 158
26.   *CGB, 132*
27.   *LE*, 29
28.   *CGB*, 157
29.   *ES*, 473
30.   *RU, 70*
31.   *TMR*, 363–364
32.   *SC*, 51
33.   "Readings from Ibn Abbad," *CP*, 751
34.   *NMI*, 150
35.   *OSM*, 262
36.   "Cables to the Ace," *CP*, 452
37.   *NSC*, 297
38.   *ES*, 456
39.   *DWL*, 237ff.

Sunday   Dawn

Breath Prayer: ES, 234
Opening Verse: "After the Night Office: Gethsemani Abbey," CP, 108, excerpted
Hymn: "Psalm," CP, 220–221
Antiphon: CGB, 131
Psalm: CGB, 131–132, excerpted
Antiphon: ES, 488
Psalm: "A Prayer to God the Father on the Vigil of Pentecost," CGB, 177–178, excerpted
Psalm Prayer: "A Prayer to God the Father on the Vigil of Pentecost," CGB, 178
Reading: NSC, 3–4, excerpted
Responsory: SJ, 361
Canticle: "The Sowing of Meanings," CP, 187–189, excerpted
Closing Prayer: TTW, 7, excerpted

Day

Breath Prayer: "Time and the Liturgy," SC, 48, excerpted
Exhortation: NSC, 81
Meditation: CGB, 157–158, excerpted
Prayer: ES, 237
Lesson: ES, 238, excerpted
Collect: LH, 68–69
Examen: CGB, 282
Kyrie: NSC, 44–46, excerpted
Benediction: HGL, 466

Dusk

Breath Prayer: ES, 487
Opening Verse: "Advent," CP, 88, excerpted
Evening Hymn: NSC, 44, excerpted
Antiphon: DWL, 178
Psalm: NSC, 296–297, excerpted
Psalm Prayer: "The Word—A Responsory," CP, 112
Epistle: HGL 115–116, excerpted
Responsory: SJ, 257
Marian Canticle: "The Evening of the Visitation," CP, 43–44
Intercessions: PP, 327–329, excerpted
Closing Prayer: ES, 473

Dark

Breath Prayer: NSC, 297
Opening Verse: "The Dark Encounter," CP, 113
Night Hymn: "The Heavenly City," CP, 147–148
Antiphon: "The Fall of Night," CP, 103
Psalm: "The Fall," DBD, 184–185
Psalm Prayer: SSM, 274, excerpted
Litany: SS, 46–47
Closing Prayer: SJ, 361–362

Monday Dawn

Breath Prayer: "Cables to the Ace: Prologue," CP, 395
Opening Verse: "In the Rain and the Sun," CP, 215
Hymn: "Song for Nobody," CP, 337–338
Antiphon: "Cables to the Ace," CP, 400
Psalm: NSC, 30–31, excerpted
Psalm Prayer: NMI, 117
Reading: CWA, 172, excerpted
Responsory: "After the Night Office: Gethsemani Abbey," CP, 109, excerpted
Canticle: "Early Legend," CP, 762–763, excerpted
Closing Prayer: NSC, 67–69

Day

Breath Prayer: LL, 159
Exhortation: LH, 121
Meditation: NSC, 19, excerpted
Prayer: ES, 48, excerpted
Lesson: NSC, 86–87
Collect: "A Whitsun Canticle," CP, 121
Examen: CGB, 146
Kyrie: NSC, 44–46, excerpted
Benediction: "Hymn for the Feast of Duns Scotus," CP, 199

Dusk

Breath Prayer: DWL, 197
Opening Verse: ES, 311
Evening Hymn: "A Whitsun Canticle," CP, 119–120, excerpted
Antiphon: SJ, 290
Psalm: NSC, 16–18, excerpted
Psalm Prayer: CGB, 43
Epistle: LL, 159, excerpted
Responsory: SJ, 18
Marian Canticle: "The Quickening of St. John the Baptist," CP, 199–200
Intercessions: PP, 327–329, excerpted
Closing Prayer: SS, 70

Dark

Breath Prayer: ES, 460, excerpted
Opening Verse: "The Captives—A Psalm," CP, 211–212
Night Hymn: "The Night of Destiny," CP, 634–635
Antiphon: RM, 20
Night Psalm: "In Silence," CP, 280–281
Psalm Prayer: "The Early Legend," CP, 757–758, excerpted
Litany: SJ, 216–217
Closing Prayer: NSC, 227

Tuesday   Dawn

Breath Prayer: *NMI*, 50
Opening Verse: "Day of a Stranger," in *Thomas Merton: Spiritual Master*, Laurence
   Cunningham, ed. (New York:Paulist Press) 218
Hymn: "How Long We Wait," *CP*, 89–90, excerpted
Antiphon: "Cables to the Ace," *CP*, 443, excerpted
Psalm: "Stranger," *CP*, 289–290
Psalm Prayer: *ES*, 423, excerpted
Reading: *WS*, 349–350
Responsory: "How Long We Wait," *CP*, 89
Canticle: "Grace's House," *CP*, 331
Closing Prayer: *SCh*, 261–262

Day

Breath Prayer: "Day of a Stranger," *DWL*, 239
Exhortation: *CT*, 195
Meditation: *SJ*, 76–77, excerpted
Prayer: *SJ*, 79
Lesson: *NSC*, 32–33, excerpted
Collect: *NSC*, 33
Examen: *HGL*, 20, excerpted
Kyrie: *NSC*, 44–46, excerpted
Benediction: *NSC*, 59–60, excerpted

Dusk

Breath Prayer: *SS*, 214–215
Opening Verse: *SJ*, 286, excerpted
Evening Hymn: "Elias—Variations on a Theme," *CP*, 244–245, excerpted
Antiphon: *HGL*, 153
Psalm: *TS*, 99–100
Psalm Prayer: *CGB*, 178, excerpted
Epistle: *HGL*, 155–156, excerpted
Responsory: *SSM*, 163
Marian Canticle: "The Blessed Virgin Mary Compared to a Window," *CP*, 46–47
Intercessions: *PP*, 327–329, excerpted
Closing Prayer: *NSC*, 231

Dark

Breath Prayer: *ES*, 196, excerpted
Opening Verse: "The Candlemas Procession," *CP*, 92
Night Hymn: "When in the Soul of the Serene Disciple," *CP*, 279–280
Antiphon: *SJ*, 360, excerpted
Night Psalm: "Evening Prayer" (Psalm 140–141), *CP*, 711–712
Psalm Prayer: *TMR*, 375
Litany: *ES*, 67, excerpted
Closing Prayer: *NSC*, 227

Wednesday Dawn

Breath Prayer: "The Dark Encounter," CP, 113, excerpted
Opening Verse: NSC, 226, excerpted
Hymn: "Song: Contemplation," CP, 157–159, excerpted
Antiphon: ES, 471
Psalm: SJ, 346
Psalm Prayer: ES, 474
Reading: CGB, 280
Responsory: "Holy Communion: The City," CP, 39–40
Canticle: "Early Legend," CP, 762
Closing Prayer: "A Whitsun Canticle," CP, 119

Day

Breath Prayer: ES, 186, excerpted
Exhortation: HGL, 92
Meditation, first paragraph: CT, 197, excerpted
Meditation, second paragraph: HGL, 259, excerpted
Meditation, third paragraph: HGL, 126
Prayer: "Whitsun Canticle," CP, 121, excerpted
Lesson: HGL, 272, excerpted
Collect: "Readings from Ibn Abbad," CP, 751
Examen: HGL, 325–326, excerpted
Kyrie: NSC, 44–46
Benediction: CT, 207

Dusk

Breath Prayer: ES, 460, excerpted
Opening Verse: "Canticle for the Blessed Virgin," CP, 163
Evening Hymn: "Hymn for the Feast of Duns Scotus," CP, 198–199
Antiphon: SSM, 508
Psalm: ES, 403, excerpted
Psalm Prayer: NMI, 232
Epistle: HGL, 156–157, excerpted
Responsory: ES, 131
Marian Canticle: "The Annunciation," CP, 284–285
Intercessions: PP, 327–329, excerpted
Closing Prayer: TS, 83

Dark

Breath Prayer: "The Night of Destiny," DBD, 72
Opening Verse: "Cables to the Ace," CP, 431
Night Hymn: "Evening," CP, 41–42
Antiphon: CT, 200
Psalm: "Be My Defender" (Psalm 4), CP, 692–693
Psalm Prayer: NSC, 81–82
Litany: NSC, 216, excerpted
Closing Prayer: NSC, 82–83

Thursday Dawn

Breath Prayer: "Song: If You Seek. . .," CP, 340
Opening Verse: *DWL*, 250
Hymn: "The Trappist Abbey: Matins," CP, 45–46, excerpted
Antiphon: "Atlas and the Fatman," CP, 691
Psalm: "O Sweet Irrational Worship," CP, 344–345
Psalm Prayer: "Atlas and the Fatman," CP, 691, excerpted
Reading: *NSC*, 60–61
Responsory: *TS*, 71
Canticle: "Song: If You Seek. . .," CP, 340–341
Closing Prayer: *ES*, 193

Day

Breath Prayer: *DWL*, 346
Exhortation: "Cables to the Ace," CP, 449–450
Meditation: *SJ*, 47, excerpted
Prayer: *ES*, 199
Lesson: *LL*, 36
Collect: *ES*, 199
Examen: *WSD*, 48
Kyrie: *NSC*, 44–46, excerpted
Benediction: *SS*, 70

Dusk

Breath Prayer: "Time and the Liturgy," *SC*, 49, excerpted
Opening Verse: "The Victory," CP, 171–172
Evening Hymn: "After Night Office—Gethsemani Abbey," CP, 108–109, excerpted
Antiphon: "Trappists Working," CP, 96
Psalm: *CGB*, 158, excerpted
Psalm Prayer: *NSC*, 67
Epistle: *HGL*, 157
Responsory: *SSM*, 163
Marian Canticle: "Canticle for the Blessed Virgin," CP, 161
Intercessions: *PP*, 327–329, excerpted
Closing Prayer: *AJ*, 318–319. Merton gave this as the closing prayer at the First
    Spiritual Summit conference in Calcutta, India.

Dark

Breath Prayer: *SC*, 93–94
Opening Verse: "St. John's Night," CP, 172
Night Hymn: "How Long We Wait," CP, 89–90, excerpted
Antiphon: *ES*, 235, excerpted
Psalm: "The Lord Is Good" (Psalm 71), CP, 775–776.
Psalm Prayer: *SSM*, 161–162
Litany: "Litany," CP, 724–725, excerpted
Closing Prayer: *AJ*, 308, excerpted

Friday

Dawn

Breath Prayer: "Spring: Monastery Farm," CP, 170
Opening Verse: "The Trappist Cemetery—Gethsemani," CP, 118
Hymn: "Early Mass," CP, 282, excerpted
Antiphon: "The Biography," CP, 104
Psalm: "Cables to the Ace," CP, 449
Psalm Prayer: "With the World in My Bloodstream," DBD, 190
Reading: CGB, 171–172
Responsory: TTW, 18
Canticle: ES, 412, excerpted
Closing Prayer: SJ, 327

Day

Breath Prayer: "Time and the Liturgy," SC, 49, excerpted
Exhortation: "The Ointment," CP, 777
Meditation: TS, 39, excerpted
Prayer: Ibid.
Lesson, first paragraph: SSM, 166–167
Lesson, second paragraph: CT, 188
Collect: LtL, 15
Examen, first paragraph: TTW, 59–60
Examen, second paragraph: ES, 311
Kyrie: NSC, 44–46, excerpted
Benediction: WSD, 24

Dusk

Breath Prayer: "Freedom as Experience," CP, 187
Opening Verse: "Senescente Mundo," CP, 222
Evening Hymn: "Earthquake" (Isaiah 52) CP, 701–703.
Antiphon: AJ, 308
Psalm: "Atlas and the Fat Man," CP, 690–691
Psalm Prayer: "The Victory," CP, 114
Epistle: HGL, 157–158
Responsory: LtL, 220
Marian Canticle: "To the Immaculate Virgin, on a Winter Night," CP, 218–219
Intercessions: PP, 327–329, excerpted
Closing Prayer: CT, 184

Dark

Breath Prayer: ES, 186
Opening Verse: "Advent," CP, 88, excerpted
Night Hymn: "Sacred Heart 2 (A Fragment—)," CP, 24
Antiphon: "The Transformation: For the Sacred Heart," CP, 176
Psalm: "Perfect Joy," CP, 896–897
Psalm Prayer: DWL, 175, excerpted
Litany: NSC, 10–13, excerpted
Closing Prayer: DWL, 175, excerpted

Saturday   Dawn

Breath Prayer: NSC, 228
Opening Verse: "Hagia Sophia" I. Dawn. The Hour of Lauds. CP, 363
Hymn: Ibid.
Antiphon: Ibid.
Psalm: Ibid., 363–364, excerpted
Psalm Verse: Ibid., 363, excerpted
Reading: Ibid., 364–365, excerpted
Responsory: Ibid., 365
Canticle: "Hagia Sophia" II. Early Morning. The Hour of Prime. CP, 365–366,
    excerpted
Closing Prayer: Ibid., 366

Day

Breath Prayer: ES, 196
Exhoration: "Hagia Sophia" III. High Morning. The Hour of Tierce. CP, 366
Meditation: Ibid., 366–367
Prayer: Ibid., 367
Lesson: Ibid., excerpted
Collect: Ibid.
Examen: "Hagia Sophia" II. Early Morning. The Hour of Prime. CP, 365, excerpted
Kyrie: NSC 44–46, excerpted
Benediction: "Hagia Sophia" II. Early Morning. The Hour of Prime. CP, 367–368

Dusk

Breath Prayer: SS 214
Opening Verse: "Hagia Sophia" III. High Morning. The Hour of Terse. CP, 368
Evening Hymn: Ibid., 368–369
Antiphon: Ibid., 369
Psalm: Ibid.
Psalm Prayer: "Hagia Sophia" IV. Sunset. The Hour of Compline. Salve Regina. CP,
    369
Epistle: Ibid., 370
Responsory: Ibid.
Marian Canticle: Ibid.
Closing Prayer: Ibid., 370–371

Dark

Entire Section: "Fire Watch," SJ, 349–362, excerpted

Postscript

Final Benediction: HGL, 110

Thomas Merton Bibliography

Letters

The Courage for Truth: Letters to Writers. Christine Bochen, ed. New York: Harcourt, Brace, 1993.

The Hidden Ground of Love: The Letters of Thomas Merton on Religious Experience and Social Concerns. William Shannon, ed. New York: Farrar, Straus, Giroux, 1985.

The Road to Joy: Letters of Thomas Merton to New and Old Friends. Robert Daggy, ed. New York: Farrar, Straus, 1989.

The School of Charity: Letters of Thomas Merton on Religious Renewal and Spiritual Direction. Brother Patrick Hart, ed. New York: Farrar, Strauss, 1990.

Journals

Conjectures of a Guilty Bystander. Garden City, NY: Doubleday, 1966.

The Journals of Thomas Merton. Patrick Hart, osco, general editor:

Volume One: 1939–1941, *Run to the Mountain.* Patrick Hart, osco, ed. San Francisco: HarperSanFrancisco, 1995.

Volume Two: 1941–1952, *Entering the Silence.* Jonathan Montaldo, ed. San Francisco: HarperSanFrancisco, 1996.

Volume Three: 1952–1960, *A Search for Solitude.* Lawrence S. Cunningham, ed. San Francisco: HarperSanFrancisco, 1996.

Volume Four: 1960–1963, *Turning Toward the World.* Victor Kramer, ed. San Francisco: HarperSanFrancisco, 1996.

Volume Five: 1963–1965, *Dancing in the Waters of Life.* Robert Daggy, ed. San Francisco: HarperSanFrancisco, 1997.

Volume Six: 19661967, *Learning to Love.* Christine Bochen, ed. San Francisco: HarperSanFrancisco, 1997.

Volume Seven: 19671968, *The Other Side of the Mountain.* Patrick Hart, osco, ed. San Francisco: HarperSanFrancisco, 1998.

The Asian Journal of Thomas Merton. Naomi Burton, James Laughlin, Patrick Hart, osco, eds. New York: New Directions, 1973.

Woods, Shore, Desert. Santa Fe: Museum Press, 1983.

Poetry

The Collected Poems of Thomas Merton. New York: New Directions, 1977.

In the Dark Before Dawn: New Selected Poems of Thomas Merton, Lynn Szabo, ed. New York: New Directions, 2005.

Books

A Thomas Merton Reader, Thomas McDonnell, ed. Garden City, NY: Image Books, 1974.

Bread in the Wilderness. New York: New Directions, 1953.

Cables to the Ace. New York: New Directions, 1968.

Conjectures of a Guilty Bystander. Garden City: Doubleday, 1966.

Contemplation in a World of Action. Garden City, NY: Image Books, 1973.

Life and Holiness. New York: Herder and Herder, 1963.

Literary Essays, Patrick Hart, osco, ed. New York: New Directions, 1981.

Love and Living, Naomi Burton Stone and Patrick Hart, osco, eds. New York: Farrar, Straus, Giroux, 1979.

New Seeds of Contemplation. New York: New Directions, 1962.

No Man Is an Island. New York: Harcourt, Brace, 1955.

Passion for Peace, William Shannon, ed. New York: Crossroad Publishing Company, 1997.

Praying the Psalms. Collegeville, MN: Liturgical Press, 1956.

Raids on the Unspeakable. New York: New Directions, 1966.

Seasons of Celebration: New York: Farrar, Straus, 1965.

Seeds of Contemplation. New York: New Directions, 1948.

The Seven Storey Mountain. New York: Image Books, 1970.

Springs of Contemplation. Notre Dame: Ave Maria Press, 1997.

The Inner Experience, William Shannon, ed. San Francisco: HarperSanFrancisco, 2003.

The New Man. New York: Farrar, Straus, 1961.

The Sign of Jonas. New York: Harcourt, Brace, 1953.

The Waters of Siloe. New York: Harcourt, Brace, 1949.

Thoughts in Solitude. New York: Farrar, Straus, 1958.

OTHER WORKS CONSULTED:

Brueggeman, Walter. *Spirituality of the Psalms.* Minneapolis: Fortress Press, 2002.

Deignan, Ann. *Mythos Gate: A Book of Poems.* Schola Press, 2000.

Storey, William. *An Everyday Book of Hours.* Chicago: Liturgy Training Publications, 2002.

Tickle, Phyllis. *The Divine Hours: Prayers for Springtime*, New York: Doubleday, 2006.

Acknowledgments

The author and publisher gratefully acknowledge the following sources from which excerpts were taken. We regret any errors and oversights and will correct them in future editions.

Reprinted by permission of The Crossroad Publishing Company:

Excerpts from *Passion for Peace: The Social Essays* by Thomas Merton, edited by William H. Shannon, copyright © 1995 by the Trustees of the Merton Legacy Trust.

Reprinted by permission of Doubleday, a division of Random House, Inc.:

Excerpts from *Conjectures of a Guilty Bystander* by Thomas Merton, copyright © 1966 by The Abbey of Gethsemani.

Excerpts from *A Thomas Merton Reader* by Thomas P. McDonnell, copyright ©1974 by The Trustees of the Merton Legacy Trust.

Reprinted by permission of Farrar, Straus, and Giroux, LLC:

Excerpts from *The Courage for Truth: The Letters of Thomas Merton to Writers* by Thomas Merton, edited by Christine M. Bochen, copyright © 1993 by the Merton Legacy Trust.

Excerpts from *The Hidden Ground of Love* by Thomas Merton, copyright © 1985 by The Merton Legacy Trust.

Excerpts from *Love and Living* by Thomas Merton, copyright © 1979 by The Trustees of the Merton Legacy Trust.

Excerpts from *The School of Charity: The Letters of Thomas Merton on Religious Renewal and Spiritual Direction* by Thomas Merton, edited by Brother Patrick Hart, copyright © 1990 by the Merton Legacy Trust.

Excerpts from *Seasons of Celebration* by Thomas Merton, copyright © 1965 by The Abbey of Gethsemani. Copyright renewed 1993 by Robert Giroux, James Laughlin, and Tommy O'Callaghan.

Excerpts from *Thoughts in Solitude* by Thomas Merton, copyright © 1958 by The Abbey of Our Lady of Gethsemani. Copyright renewed 1988 by the Merton Legacy Trust.

Reprinted by permission of Harcourt, Inc.:

Excerpts from *No Man Is an Island* by Thomas Merton, copyright ©1955 by The Abbey of Our Lady of Gethsemani and renewed 1983 by the Trustees of The Merton Legacy Trust.

Excerpts from *The Seven Storey Mountain* by Thomas Merton, copyright 1948 by Harcourt, Inc., and renewed 1976 by the Trustees of The Merton Legacy Trust.

Excerpts from *The Sign of Jonas* by Thomas Merton, copyright 1953 by The Abbey of Our Lady of Gethsemani and renewed 1981 by the Trustees of The Merton Legacy Trust.

Excerpts from *The Waters of Siloe*, copyright 1949 by Thomas Merton and renewed 1977 by the Trustees of the Merton Legacy Trust.

Kathleen Deignan is an educator, theologian, and composer.  A sister of the Congregation of Notre Dame, she holds a master's degree in Christian spirituality and a doctorate in historical theology from Fordham University. Deignan is a professor of Religious Studies at Iona College in New Rochelle, New York, where she founded and directs the Iona Spirituality Institute. She is composer in residence for Schola Ministries which has produced over a dozen of her recordings of original sacred songs (www.ScholaMinistries.org).

Deignan has written numerous articles in the area of classical and contemporary spirituality, particularly on the legacy of Thomas Merton. She is also the editor of *When the Trees Say Nothing*, a collection of Merton's writings on nature.

Internationally known artist John Giuliani is an American  spiritual and cultural treasure. His widely acclaimed works, which typically blend Native American images with traditional Christian iconography, are displayed in churches across the United States. Giuliani oversees The Benedictine Grange, a spiritual center in West Redding, Connecticut, which he founded in 1977.